BY THE SAME AUTHOR.

MEMOIRS OF
THE ROYAL ARTILLERY BAND

Its Origin, History and Progress

(An Account of the Rise of Military Music in England)

14 Illustrations

PRESS OPINIONS.

The Standard says:—"In MEMOIRS OF THE ROYAL ARTILLERY BAND .... will be found much interesting and out of the way information concerning the origin and development of military music in England. . . . The book ... includes a mass of details."

The Daily Chronicle says:—" Mr. Farmer has not only written an interesting history of the band, but has gathered together some quaint old lore relating to the earliest military music in England."

The Times says:—"A record to which Mr. Farmer has devoted considerable research."

The Referee says:—"There should be many readers. . . . Mr. Farmer would seem to have swept into his book every item of information."

The Broad Arrow says:—"A remarkable work. . . . replete with information of a valuable and interesting kind, and should secure a good sale and many readers, even outside of military circles. . . . Not only interesting, but instructive from the first page to the last."

The R.A. Institution Proceedings says:—"A very intelligible and interesting history of the R.A. Band, hitherto veiled in darkness. . . . The book, deserves a large circulation."

The Musical Times says:—"We have nothing but praise for the book. . . . which shows a considerable amount of original research. . . . . Furnishes much information on a branch of music that is comparatively little known."

The Orchestral Times says:—"A most exhaustive history. . . . We must compliment the author on the manner in which he has placed the material he has unearthed, also for the excellent style in which the book has been produced."

The Musical Record says:—"This work will be thankfully received. . . . Will appeal not only to musicians, but even to the general public."

The Military Mail says:—" A volume which should go a long way towards building up that history of British Military Music which is much needed, and which we should say he (Mr. Farmer) is fully qualified to write."

LONDON: WILLIAM REEVES, 93 CHARING CROSS ROAD, W.C.

To My Friend

E. A. REYNOLDS

And " The Rank and File " of

Army Bands.

FOREWORD.

TO write a general history of military music, one embracing a continuous and coherent account of its progress, is no easy task; for the simple reason that its development has not been general, but has proceeded on different lines in different countries.

The growing interest in the subject manifested in Britain during recent years is perhaps not the least encouraging feature noticeable in connection with the spread of general culture, the best wind-band combinations now attracting vast audiences on concert platforms formerly considered the exclusive monopoly of the grand orchestra.

There is on all sides, an acquaintance with music, vocal or instrumental: and whilst much of this may be of only an elementary character, there is, and that more widely diffused than is perhaps generally known, a very high standard of musical culture indeed abroad.

During the past half-century, literature in all other branches of musical art has grown enormously and is still being poured out at a bewildering rate—yet works treating of military music, of its history, or of its theory, are conspicuously rare, and may be counted almost on the fingers of one hand.

True, the existing traces of its beginnings and development are meagre, and even what is to be gleaned on the subject is exceedingly difficult of access. The reader need only note the authorities cited in the present volume—all rare, or comparatively rare, works—in order to satisfy himself that the story of military music is only to be found strewn about among the pages of history in what might appear to be a loose and haphazard manner.

One has to seek among the highways and by-ways of literature for data; memoirs and autobiography, official documents and anecdote, annals and records of all kinds, doings in themselves entirely unconnected with the subject of music, but yet furnishing some trace, some tiny fragment of information, helpful to the author. His materials are scattered over several centuries; involving much painstaking research, much diving into dusty and almost forgotten corners, much wading through ponderous tomes, which in the end yield perhaps one scant paragraph of any practical use to the inquirer, nay, sometimes even rewarding him with nothing for his pains.

The representative military band of the present day has reached a high state of executive excellence; its constitution, already rich, is ever expanding; while its repertory, with certain slight reservations, knows no boundaries.

France has always taken the lead in military music. Its archives furnish many important documents bearing on schemes for the art's betterment, in which we find associated all the principal musical names of the day. This year (1912) France is promoting a grand international contest for bands. -Large prizes are offered, one for £500, and it is confidently hoped that all the nations will send representatives.

Austria and Germany boast some really fine bands, although—and this particularly is the case in the latter country—one feels that artistic considerations often yield to those utilitarian.

Much attention has been devoted to wind band music in Italy—the service combinations being rarely below fifty in numbers, including the fanfare. The Italian cavalry has no music. All the large cities boast very fine organisations of seventy to eighty musicians, which, while they are under municipal control, enjoy wide European fame.

The Continent is now so easy of access and international exhibitions so frequent, undertakings in which good open-air music occupies so important and conspicuous a place as to necessitate usually a special bureau of management all to itself, that we are now more or less familiar with most of the bands of European reputation.

But the Western hemisphere has not been inactive.

For although new or comparatively new countries do not, by reason of their want of leisured classes, cultivate art in anything like the same degree as do the nations of older civilisation, yet we find on the American continent several really capital wind instrumental combinations.

America itself has at least half-a-dozen good bands; mostly proprietary. Among government organisations the band of the Washington Marines, under Mr. Santlemann, stands easily foremost. Mexico, too, has a very fine band in that of its Artillery stationed at Mexico city. They are seventy-five strong, the instrumentation being on the French model, and embracing the entire family of saxophones. They play an up-to-date repertoire and give capital renderings of such writers as Puccini and Saint-Saëns.

Another very interesting body of performers is the band of the Filipino Scouts, fifty strong. They play entirely from memory, thus limiting the extent of their repertory, but, having regard to the conditions under which musical studies must be pursued in their country, the finished manner in which these little fellows render their fairly diversified programmes is little short of amazing. They show a decided predilection for ornate music, which is, I suppose, only natural to players who have to commit to memory.

Owing to a variety of causes military band music has increased enormously in popular favour in the British Isles during the past twenty years.

The advent of the annual exhibition, the popularity

of the sea-side holiday, Sunday concerts—winter and summer—playing in the public parks—all have contributed to render wind band music indispensable: whilst no gala, flower-show, cricket match, or even race meeting is considered quite complete without its band.

A marked advance, too, is to be noticed in the programmes now performed. France and Germany have long included in their open-air band performances excerpts from the best masters, from works of that class which merits, and is distinguished by, the term *classical*; but it is only of comparatively recent years that any great strides in this direction are found in Britsh bands, such improvements, or attempt at improvement, being often made only with great diffidence, and this for a very odd reason, the fear of incurring the censure of those who, if they do not altogether disapprove of military bands, at any rate discourage all serious work by those organisations and view such efforts with an amused and superior air—as one might Bach on an harmonium or Wagner on a tin-whistle.

And here we may note that there has of late sprung up a school of *reactionnaires* who raise their voice—at times a pretty harsh, loud and offensive voice, too—against what they are pleased to term the pretensions of the military conductor. They deplore the performance by military bands of the best musical works, the maltreatment of the most noble productions of art. "Where is the rush of the violins?" "I miss the sweep

of the strings" are examples of their slang. They
would prohibit the military band altogether, to them
it is sacrilege, the conductor anathema, they rend their
garments and go in sackcloth because of his iniquities.
In short, they would relegate the military musician to
his original and proper place, playing marches at the
head of his regiment; or at best to attendance at country
fairs, where his artistic depredations should be restricted
to the Coote and Tinney polka and quadrille nicely out
of tune.

With the very best desire to be agreeable and accom-
modating, we venture to believe that the military band
is capable of much higher things. It seems nothing
short of disgraceful that such views as those referred
to should in this progressive age gain admission to the
columns of the public press.

A really good assortment of wind instruments, per-
fectly intoned, the proportions being just and nicely
balanced, and giving an artistic and intelligible rendering of a good work, is, to the discerning auditor,
such as is to be found by the thousand at a summer
evening performance in Hyde Park, much to be pre-
ferred to a poor rendering of the same or a similar
work by a second-rate organist or inferior orchestra,
whose piteous plea is that theirs is "the instrument for
which the composer designed his work," wretched and
commonplace though the rendition be.

In spite of all ill-natured abuse and invective; in
despite even of ridicule, responsible and educated military musicians are not likely to be deterred or in any

way influenced by the diatribist. They will be guided solely by consideration for the dignity of their art; for the steady and certain advance of the peculiar branch which they have made their own; modestly, yet firmly, believing that it is with them either to ennoble or to degrade that branch, and that by setting themselves lofty ideals and by the earnest pursuit of only the highest aims, they may contribute to real progress, as well as to the diffusion of the joys of music among the people; having special and solicitous regard too, for that vast majority of the people who find little or no opportunity of hearing the best orchestras.

Music—so frequently likened to medicine—should always be of the best. Bad drugs, 'tis said, only aggravate an ailment and are worse than none at all. So with music. If the carping critic would effect reforms in military band programmes, would place limitations on our possibilities *for evil*, then we say: "Very well, delete the bad, excise the musical slang and have only *good* music." Do not force us to "deck the lovely messenger of peace" in cap and bells, in rouge, powder and pompons.

It is recorded that during the "hundred days" Napoleon created Cherubini a Chevalier of the Legion d'Honneur—*as leader of the band of the National Guards of Paris.* At a lecture delivered quite recently at the Royal United Service Institute it was suggested that by certain reductions in the numbers of our army bands a saving of 7,000 men might be effected! Another type of the reactionary.

It is interesting and gratifying to know that the importance of military music as a factor in the nation's existence, as a contributory element to its joys—and sometimes to its sorrows—is not wholly lost sight of in Britain.

Measures have at different times been adopted to encourage original composition for military bands. In 1872 the Alhambra management offered a prize of £200 for the best fantasia. The committee of adjudicators, presided over by Sir Arthur Sullivan, declared M. van Herzeele, a Belgian, the winner.

During recent years considerable impetus has been given to progress in the same direction by the action of the Worshipful Company of Musicians, who, for the coronation of the late King Edward, and again for that of His present Majesty, offered substantial prizes for the best coronation march; and stipulated, among other conditions, that the competing works should be scored for a military band.

Again, in 1909, this same company offered five prizes for original military band compositions moulded in the higher forms, an offer which had the very gratifying result of attracting the attention of several native musicians of note, thus promoting and stimulating production.

Furthermore, it presents annually a medal to the best all-round student of the two representative training schools for military music, the Royal Military School at Kneller Hall and the Royal Naval School at Eastney; thus placing these service institutions on an equal footing, as regards recognition by the ancient guild, with the great civil schools, the R.A.M., R.C.M. and G.S.M.

At Kneller Hall composition is encouraged by. the offer yearly of a prize for the best original work in the form of an overture, and here it is significant to note that the competitors sometimes exhibit an acquaintance with such advanced classic models as those represented by Brahms. (Mention is made of this latter fact merely as indicating the spirit of inquiry abroad among these young musicians.)

The Royal Naval School of Music is a particularly important institution, over four hundred students being under daily instruction. It supplies the entire navy with musicians—a truly gigantic undertaking—its obligations differing considerably thereby from those of the sister institution at Kneller Hall.

Mr. Farmer has already many claims to the gratitude of musicians by his very interesting work on the Royal Artillery Band, and this latest contribution to military musical history can only increase these claims and enhance his reputation as an industrious and intelligent writer on that subject.

Any light thrown on the very obscure history of military music can but prove acceptable to the musically curious, and the present volume will not be least welcome to those who, like myself, have, as students, so frequently deplored the paucity of works treating

of military music; who have had at times to plod
laboriously through whole volumes in order to verify
some short but important statement on which the mind
lingered in doubt.

A. WILLIAMS.

LONDON, *January, 1912.*

PREFACE.

"A history of British military music is much needed."—
"Musical Times" (1897).

"The subject of military music . . . . has been strangely
neglected in Germany and England."—W. BARCLAY SQUIRE in
Grove's "Dictionary."

"It is a curious fact that . . . . little or no attention is
given to military bands, either in . . . . musical dictionaries or
encyclopædias."—ROBERT A. MARR in "Music and Musicians."

"While historians revelled in descriptions of the grandeur
of ecclesiastical compositions, of the music of the princely
palaces or the royal playhouses, the music of the people has
been passed over with almost contemptuous indifference . . . .
as if they were . . . . ashamed to mention the poor cousin who
found inspiration in the open air, or 'went a-soldiering.' "—
J. A. KAPPEY in "Military Music."

———

THESE few extracts, serving in the van, as it
were, may show how real is the complaint of
musical *littérateurs*, that England, the land of
such great military fame, should have no history of its
military music. Not long ago, a well-known authority
on military bands in America, Major F. A Mahan,
contributed a series of articles on "Military Band History and Organisation" to the "Military Service
Journal" (U.S.A.), in which he apologised for so many

references to French bands, explaining that France was the only country that possessed any literature on the subject. His survey, which even made reference to Austria and Germany, ignored England entirely.

To a certain extent his remarks were correct, although it seems strange that Major Mahan had not heard of the present author's "Memoirs of the Royal Artillery Band: An Account of the Rise of Military Music in England" (1904), a work that had even been reviewed in American papers, and much of it reproduced (without permission) in the pages of the "Metronome."

However, as I have remarked, Major Mahan had real cause for his complaint. Take Engel's "Literature of National Music"; the only works he mentions, relative to our subject, are Kastner's "Manuel Général de la Musique Militaire" (1848) and his "Chants de l'Armée Français" (1855). Matthew, in his "Literature of Music," refers only to the first book of Kastner and Day's "Catalogue of Instruments at the Royal Military Exhibition." Grove's "Dictionary" enumerates the foregoing and adds Perrin's brochure on "Military Bands" (1863), and the present author's "Memoirs of the Royal Artillery Band" (1904), which is referred to as "an excellent book of its kind." In Breitkopf and Härtel's "International Anthology of Musical Books," the last-named work alone is mentioned. There is no need therefore to apologise for the appearance of the present work, which, with the author's earlier book, are the only works on this subject in the English language.

For special information concerning military band instrumentation and arrangement in England, the following works may be consulted: J. Clarke's "Catalogue of Wind Instruments" (185-), R. Porteous's "Bandmasters' Atlas" (1854), Mandel's "Textbook on the Instrumentation of Military Bands" (about 1860), and his "System of Music" (1863), Tamplini's "The Bandsman," Palgrave Simpson's "Bandmaster's Guide" and Griffiths's "The Military Band."

The history and organisation of French bands may be found in Kastner's two books already mentioned, Neukomm's "Histoire de la Musique Militaire" (1889), Perrin's "Military Bands" (1863), Oscar Commetant's "La Musique de la Garde Républicaine" (1894), and the "Journal Spécial de Musique Militaire," a periodical founded as far back as 1864.

Wieprecht's reorganisation of Prussian bands is to be seen in Kalkbrenner's "Wilhelm Wieprecht: sein Leben und Werken" (1882). The same author's "Die Organisation der Militairmusikchòre aller Lander" (1884) gives valuable information concerning the organization of the world's military bands.

Wind instruments and their development may be consulted in Kappey's "Military Music," Rose's "Talks with Bandsmen," Day's "Catalogue of Instruments" (1891), Engel's "Musical Instruments of all Countries" (1869) and his "Descriptive Catalogue of Musical Instruments," Mendel's "Lexikon" and Grove's "Dictionary."

Historical records of several of our "staff" bands

are contained in Marr's "Music and Musicians" (1887) and his "Music for the People" (1889), and also in "The Regiment" for 1907 by the present author.

A chronicle of military band news, besides numerous articles on military music, biographies of well-known bandmasters and instrumentalists, may be found in the following journals: "British Bandsman," "British Musician," "Orchestral Times," Boosey's "Military Journal," Hawkes's "Musical Progress" and Besson's Journal."

H. GEORGE FARMER.

CONTENTS.

CHAPTER I.

EARLY ENGLAND.

CHAPTER II.

REVIVAL OF THE MILITARY ART.

CHAPTER III.

MILITARY MUSIC (1500-1700).

CHAPTER IV.

HAUTBOYS.

CHAPTER V.

BANDS OF MUSIC.

CHAPTER VI.

TURKISH MUSIC.

CHAPTER VII.

THE INFLUENCE OF THE FRENCH REVOLUTION.

CHAPTER VIII.

Forty Years' Peace.

CHAPTER IX.

Reorganisation.

CHAPTER X.

The Renaissance.

ILLUSTRATIONS.

MILITARY MUSIC AND ITS STORY.

CHAPTER I.

EARLY ENGLAND.

(The sound) of trumpet and of drum,
That makes the warrior's stomach come;
Whose noise whets valour sharp, like beer
By thunder turned to vinegar;
(For if you hear a trumpet sound or drum beat
Who has not a month's mind to combat?)
—BUTLER's "*Hudibras.*"

OUR pagan forefathers knew nothing of these wonderful things in "Hudibras." The learned J. F. Rowbotham has shown us how, in the dim ages of the past, long before civilization's dawn, primitive man marvelled at the sound of the drum, and concluded it to be the voice of a spirit. In the process of time a regular cult grew, and the drum became a particular object of worship. Like the ark of the Hebrews, it was taken into battle "to give victory over enemies," and the warrior had but to rub it on his

1

2

thighs, and he was immediately endowed with irresistible strength, whilst the voice of the god or spirit
was found most efficacious in creating fear and dismay
in his enemies.

At a later stage of development, the horn arrives,
and man finds its frightening power far more potent
than his fetish, the drum. Martial music becomes a
separate function, and the horn its first exponent, by
virtue of its special value in "scaring the foe."[1]

The horn, then, is the prototype of our modern military trumpet. It frequently occurs in Greek art, where
it serves to distinguish the barbarians from the Greeks
who used the trumpet, and is mentioned by both Greek
and Latin poets in their accounts of primitive wars.

When it was that the Greeks adopted the trumpet
is not quite certain. That Homer was acquainted with
this rare contrivance we may safely conjecture,
although he never refers to it in his heroic battle scenes,
except as a simile. But, of course, trumpets were in
use ages before this by the Egyptians, a nation far
advanced in a civilization which surpassed anything
the ancient world ever arrived at. With the Egyptians
military music had an important place, their chief instruments being the trumpet and drum, which, says
Sir J. Gardner Wilkinson,[2] were common about the sixteenth century before our era. Both of these instruments were utilized to regulate and enliven the march,

[1] Rowbotham, "History of Music," 1885.
[2] Wilkinson, "The Ancient Egyptians," 1833.

but signals appear to have been given upon the trumpet alone. In the many representations of their battles, we find that the trumpeter's post is generally at the head of his corps, and the drummer, when playing on the march, may be seen stationed in the centre of the column, or near the standard bearers. The trumpet and drum also combined in forming a band, when they marched in the van; and curiously enough there is a representation of some troops defiling past, with the band drawn upon one side, as is the custom in modern armies.

Returning to the Greeks, we find that the drum did not find favour with them for military purposes, the flute being their special marching instrument. For although they used the trumpet for signalling, and Ælian tells us that one was appointed to each company, they considered its tone too inspiring and likely to make the soldiers impetuous, whilst the soothing tones of the flute during the march and exercises kept the troops cool and firm.[3]

The Hebrews seemed to have relied specially upon the trumpet in their wars. There is a reference to it in that part of the so-called Mosaic ordinances, which is known as the "priests' code," collated about the fifth century before our era. The passage is—"And if ye go to war in your land against the enemy that oppresseth you, then ye shall blow an alarm with the trumpets, etc"

---

[3] "Tactics of Ælian" (translated by Bingham, 1616).

The Romans, a race of fighting men, regarded military music as seriously as any other branch of the art. They had quite a host of warlike instruments, the most important of which were the tuba, or straight trumpet, the buccina, or curved trumpet, the lituus, or small trumpet, and the cornu, or horn. The performers on these instruments were called Æneatores. Every troop of horse and every maniple, if not every century of foot, had either a trumpet or horn, or both. They were employed for signals of every description in war. The lituus appears to have been the cavalry trumpet, and the buccina was used to direct the movements of troops detached from camp. These instruments may have been used for marching music, at least Æneatores march in front of the army on the Column of Antonius and the Arch of Constantine.[4]

Now that we come to our own islands, we have to turn back the pages of history, for when the legions of that great civilization—the Roman Empire—came to these shores, they found themselves confronted by a race similar to the Gauls, whom they designated "barbarians." The Britons were a very warlike race, but indifferently skilled in arms, and made very little impression on the disciplined army of Rome. We are told that they began their attacks with taunting songs and deafening howls, accompanied by the blowing of a great number of horns and trumpets, which, says Polybius, quite terrified the invaders. Several instru-

---

⁴Guhl and Koner, "Life of the Greeks and Romans," 1877.

ments of this class have been found in Ireland, a
country rich in Celtic antiquities, and considered by
many writers to be Celtic.[5] They are preserved at the
Royal Irish Academy at Dublin, and are of considerable size, having the embouchure at the side, like the
Ashantee war-horns in the British Museum.

It was the custom in those remote times to enter
battle with a war-song. The Britons would shout
their "Armed Confederacy of Britain," just as the
Saxons did their "Song of Odin."[6] The so-called
Welsh martial music of to-day no doubt breathes the
same spirit as that of the ancient Britons. As Sir J. G.
Ouseley has said : "Probably no race of men has preserved so much, unaltered, from the great storehouse
of the past as these Cambro-Britons; and it is, therefore, not unreasonable to conclude that in their oldest
tunes we may have the remains of what was anciently
the music of this country long before the Roman
invasion under Julius Cæsar."[7]

It was the marches—"The Men of Harlech," "Captain Morgan's March" and "Come to Battle," that led
Dr. Crotch to say that the military music of the Welsh
was "superior to that of any other nation."[8]

The martial music of the Saxons and Danes seems
to have been much upon the same plan as that of the

---

[5] Wakeman, "Irish Antiquities," 1842.
[6] Meyrick, "Ancient Armour."
[7] Naumann, "History of Music."
[8] Crotch, "Specimens of Various Styles of Music," etc.

Britons. The horn was the chief warlike instrument of the Saxon. The reference to it in the poem, "Beowulf," is sufficient evidence of its use in the fifth century.

> They away hurried bitter and angry
> The instant they heard the war-horn sing.

It is also mentioned in later Anglo-Saxon glossaries, so that we may come to the conclusion that although Tacitus tells us that they marched to battle to the sound of their own voices, yet they were collected in the first instance by the sound of the horn. There is a drawing in the MS. of Prudentius which seems to represent a sort of military dance or sham fight, two warriors being engaged in combat to the music of the horn.[9] "Besides the horn," says Strutt, "they had a trumpet," an example of which he shows from an old manuscript, and on the side of it is written—"When the trumpet ceases to sound, the sword is returned to the scabbard."[10] We may take this as the climax to Kipling's line:

> Blow the bugle, draw the sword.
> —"Ford o'Cabul River."

With the Danes, also, the call to arms was by the sound of the trumpet or horn. The ancient ballad, "Hardyknute,"[1] refers to the horn that "ne'er sounds

---

[9] Strutt, "Sports and Pastimes," 1833.
[10] Strutt, "Manners and Customs, etc., of England," 1775.
[1] Percy, "Relics of Ancient Poetry."

in peace," and in the "History of Charles and Grymer, Swedish Kings," we find: "All instantly fly to arms, and everyone prepares himself for battle; the trumpet sounds, and each warrior is accoutred." Grose says that several trumpets have been found in England, generally supposed to have been Danish. He gives an illustration of one over five feet in length.[2]

When William the Conqueror sailed from the Dive for the Sussex shores, his ships "resounded with music."[3] The army was accompanied by "minstrels," one of whom named Taillefer, having begged leave to lead the van, advanced to battle, singing the "Song of Roland," the Normans repeating the burden of the song, with shouts of "Dieu Aide!" And Taillefer was not simply a bard, but a valiant soldier. The sort of hero that Thomas Hood had in mind:

> Methinks I see the bounding bard
> Clad like his chief in steely garb.
> —"Decline of Chivalry."

He began the onset by slaying a Saxon standard bearer. Another likewise went down before his mighty sword. But a third overpowered him, and Taillefer left his song unfinished. In the poetical narratives of the battle of Hastings there are frequent allusions to boisines[4] and horns, especially in "Roman de Rou."

The name of "minstrel" came with the Normans,

---

[2] Grose, "Military Antiquities," 1801.
[3] Freeman, "History of the Norman Conquest," 1869.
[4] The boisine (from buccina) was a large, crooked trumpet.

and was the designation given to all who practised
the musical profession. The king and nobility had
their minstrels, and among them a certain number of
trumpeters. Indeed, the trumpet, says Kappey,[5] with
its bright and incisive tone, was "annexed" exclu-
sively for the use of kings and nobles. Trumpeters
had the rank of officers, wore the feather of nobility
in their caps, and were provided with horses and
grooms. They acted as heralds, and were required to
play brilliant tunes, which we know to-day as
"flourishes" or "fanfares," for special occasions.

When the king and nobles took to the field in time
of war, they were accompanied by their trumpeters,
upon whom they depended for the direction of military
movements and the enlivenment of the camp and
march, for under the feudal array, and even under
the mercenary system prior to the Crusades, trumpeters
or other musicians were never definitely attached to
bodies of troops. That music played an important
part in the martial display of these times may be
gathered from an incident at the siege of Rochester in
1088 under William I. When Bishop Eudes was
forced to surrender, he obtained the king's permission
to quit the city with all arms and horses. Not satis-
fied with this, he further endeavoured to seek the
favour, that the king's military music should not sound
their triumphant "fanfares" during the capitulation.
But William angrily refused, saying that he would not

[5] Kappey, "Military Music."

make the concession for a thousand gold marks. So, when the rebellious Normans marched out of Rochester, they did so with colours lowered, and to the sound of the king's trumpets.

In the public expenditures made in the fifth year of Edward I (1276) there is payment to one named Robert, styled "King of the Minstrels," being chief of them, apparently, for military service,[6] and in 1292, there is a Randolph, the king's trumpeter, who had also held a similar post under Henry III. In 1310, a charge is made, for Janino la Chevretter (bagpiper), Roger the Trumpeter, and Janino le Nakerer (kettle-drummer), all of them King's Minstrels, who are paid sixty shillings. The Minstrels of Edward III comprised five trumpeters, two clarions (small trumpets), five pipers, three waits (a kind of oboe) and four others,[7] who held their appointments for life "by letters patent," each being paid sevenpence halfpenny daily, besides other rewards, such as in 1359, when forty pounds were given to the king's herald and his companions the minstrels for attending the tournament at Smithfield.[8] King Henry V had seventeen minstrels at court, ten of whom were trumpeters. They accompanied him "with all his martial train" to France, and the part they played in England's glorious victories at

[6] Scott, "History of the British Army," 1868.
[7] Hawkins, "History of Music," 1776.
[8] "Brantingham Roll," 1370.

Crecy and Agincourt was not forgotten by the
chroniclers.

Horns and trumpets were the only instruments of
martial music, until the Crusaders returned with newer
and better ideas from the East. Richard of Devizes
tells us how, when Richard "Cœur de Lion" harangued
his soldiers at Messina, he directed that "every man,
according to military discipline, be disposed in line in
exact array, and on the third day, at the sound of the
horn, let them follow me." Thus it is clear that the
horn was a signalling instrument, yet we are told that
the troops were led to battle by the trumpet. The same
chronicler says: "The King of England proceeds in
arms; the terrible standard of the dragon is borne in
front unfurled, while behind the king the sound of
the trumpet excites the army."[9]

With regard to signals by horn or trumpet, it
appears that no distinct calls were sounded, but were
dependent for their significance on orders previously
issued,[10] as we find in the chronicle of Geoffrey de
Vinsauf (concerning the Crusade of Richard I): "It
had been resolved by common consent that the sounding of six trumpets in three different parts of the army
should be a signal for a charge, etc."[1] This might be
noted in connection with Mr. W. Barclay Squire's statement (Grove's "Dictionary"), that it is in the thirteenth

---

Bohn's "Chronicles of the Crusades."
Fortescue, "History of the British Army."
Bohn's "Chronicles of the Crusades."

century that we first find undoubted evidence of the
sounding of trumpets in a field of battle as a signal
for attack! There is another interesting item in the
same chronicle, that is worth while quoting, as it points
to what may be taken for a fanfare of trumpets *in
harmony*. The account reads: "Meanwhile the trumpets blew, and their sounds being harmoniously
blended, there arose a kind of discordant concord of
notes, whilst the sameness of the sounds being continued, the one followed the other in mutual succes-
sion, and the notes which had been lowered were again
resounded."[3]

---

[1] Bohn's "Chronicles of the Crusades."

CHAPTER II.

REVIVAL OF THE MILITARY ART.

MILITARY music did not assume any definite shape until the time of the Crusades. When the soldiers of the Cross came in contact with the Saracens, they found a civilization vastly superior to their own; and that great intellectual ferment which succeeded those terrible religious convulsions, leading to the revival of learning in Europe, had its roots in Saracenic culture. Even the renaissance of the military art was born of the Crusades. One factor at least —the military band, which was no doubt copied from the Saracens,[3] will claim attention here. The Hon. J. W. Fortescue tells us[4] that in the Saracen army minstrels were employed to indicate a rallying point; "for although at ordinary times the standards sufficed to show men the places of their leaders, yet in the dust

---

[3] Michaud, "History of the Crusades."
[4] Fortescue, "History of the British Army," 1899.

13

of battle these were often hidden from sight; and it was therefore the rule to gather the minstrels around the standards and bid them blow and beat strenuously and unceasingly during the action. The silence of the band was taken as a proof that a battalion had been broken and that the colours were in danger." The fashion lasted so long that even in the twelfth century the musicians were still under the immediate command of the "ensigns," and in battle pictures were depicted drawn up at a safe distance from the fight, energetically playing.

The musical display of the Saracens is described by one Crusader[5] as comprising trumpets, clarions, horns, pipes, drums, cymbals—a prodigious array, creating a horrible noise and clamour. "They did this," says the chronicler, "to excite their spirit and courage, for the more violent the clamour became the more bold they were for the fray." This terrific ensemble seemed at first very strange to the Crusaders, and led to much confusion in their ranks, but gradually they came to see what a valuable adjunct to the military art the band of music was, and lost little time in adopting it. One thing especially took the Crusaders' fancy, and that was the Saracen side drum and kettledrum, which were then unknown in European military music. They were introduced into our service as the tabour and

[5] Geoffrey de Vinsauf, "Chronicles of the Crusades" (Bohn's Library).

naker, and are frequently mentioned in the accounts of the Crusades. Thus it became the custom to employ bands of minstrels for the army, in addition to the trumpeters and others attached to the suites of the king and the nobility.

About this time the break-up of the roving minstrel class was in full progress. Among these poor Bohemians, pestered on one hand by the anathema of the Church and hounded on the other by the stern arm of the law, we find the more staid of them settling down in the large towns and forming themselves in "guilds," to become vested later with the respectable office of corporation minstrels[6] known in those days as "waits."[7] Others of more robust type joined the military bands,[8] for although, like their confrères who settled in the towns, they were anxious to receive the rights of the Church and the protection of the law by assuming a "respectable" vocation, they still hankered after the free and adventurous life they had been used to, and in those days of almost incessant wars and campaigning, the military service held out splendid inducements. Whatever they received by way of regular payment, sundry "rewards" were

---

[6] Kappey, "Grove's Dictionary of Music" (article, Wind Band).

[7] These waits were sometimes called upon for warlike services as in the case of the 'waits' of Norwich who accompanied Sir Francis Drake on board his ship in the days of the Spanish Armada.—"Musical Times," June, 1907.

[8] Naumann, "History of Music."

always expected for special services, to which there is
a reference in an old fifteenth century (?) ballad made
on the battle of Otterbourne.[9]

> Wherefore schote archars, for my sake
> And let scharpe arowes flee:
> Mynstrells playe up for your waryson (reward)
> And well quyt it shall be.

To judge by the old English chronicles, these minstrels were undoubtedly held in high estimation, and
their contribution to the battle's success was invariably
recorded. When the Scots suffered defeat at the hands
of Edward III on Hallidon Hill (1333) the musical
part of the programme is described by a ballad
historian:

> This was do with merry sowne .
> With pipes, trompes and tabers thereto
> And loud clarionnes thei blew also.["]

The minstrels that accompanied the king's army to
France held fine positions, ranked as officers and paid
twelve pence per diem,[1] a big sum in those days, and
at the triumphal entry into Calais in 1347 they combined in a grand military concert (says Froissart) of
"trompes, de tambours, de nacaires, de chalemies et de
muses," to greet the king   That this was martial music
par excellence is borne out by Chaucer in his account

'Percy, "Relics of Ancient English Poetry."

" Grose, "Military Antiquities," 1801.

'*Ibid.*

of the tournament in the "Knight's Tale," where these
instruments are classed with those "that in the battle
blow bloody sounds." What sort of music these minstrels played must remain a mystery to us. At best it
may have been popular dance tunes or ballads,
assuredly with a vast display of drum.

We may infer, however, that their main business was
to create "noise." Indeed, this was the name given
at this period to a combination of musical instruments
in performance,[2] and certainly no libel in this case.

With the dawn of the sixteenth century came the
renaissance of the art of war in Europe, and soldiering
was being gradually consolidated into a system.
Kings and princes began to lay the foundations of
their standing armies, and great attention was given
to military administration, drilling, equipment and
everything appertaining to martial pomp and display.
The old system of employing minstrels during a campaign had fallen into desuetude. Armies were adopting precise codes of musical signals, whilst the march
in exact rhythm, accompanied by musical instruments,
was now carefully taught. All this necessitated
properly trained musicians who could operate with the
particular units to which they belonged.

---

[2] As late as 1650, there is a letter from Popham to Blake,
asking for trumpeters for the fleet, and particularly a "complete noise" for their own ship.—Grove, "Dictionary of
Music" (article, Band).

As the old court trumpeters served on horseback,
the custom arose of looking upon trumpet music as
being specially appropriate to the cavalry, not only
for signalling but also for the march, and eventually
became regularly attached to it.[3]   In the companies of
"foot" the side-drum was retained for conveying
commands, and in company with the bagpipe provided
excellent marching music.   Hitherto, the only musicians employed in the army were those attached to the
suites of the great military officers—the Marshal, High
Constable, Captains and Lieutenant Generals, etc.
They were now allotted, in addition, to sections of
infantry and cavalry, two drummers to each company
of the former, and one trumpeter to each troop of the
latter, who received special rates of pay.

Almost to the close of the fifteenth century, the
trumpet appears to have been the only instrument used
in signalling for both infantry and cavalry.   Even
when Machiavelli wrote his "Art of War" (1521), there
was still a feeling in favour of retaining the instrument for both services.   Although he gives the side-
drum a most important place, he recommends that a
trumpeter be attached to commanding officers of
cavalry and infantry to announce all commands during
the fight.   We have already seen that precise musical
and rhythmical signals by trumpet and drum were
practically unknown.   Orders were made known to

---

[3] Kappey, Grove's "Dictionary of Music" (article, Wind
Band).

4

troops by a recognized system of moving the colours and standard, or viva voce. Trumpets often sounded to convey an order, but this would be determined upon beforehand, as we find in Froissart—"Au premier son

Fig. 1.

TRUMPETER (SIXTEENTH CENTURY). BY JOST AMMAN.

de sa trompette ou s'appareillât, au second on s'armât, et au tiers son montât à cheval et partit." A similar order to this may be seen in the " Rules and Ordinances for the War" (1544).

With the revival of classical learning came the revival of study in the art of war, and the warlike treatises of the fifteenth and sixteenth century simply teem with excerpts from Ælian, Vegetius and others. Here they found that the pagans of old had a regular code of musical signals, by which certain military movements could be performed. There were occasions when the human voice could not be heard, and the standards even were of little value in the dust of battle. But a certain note or melody that would be understood by troops as meaning a certain movement, was a great advantage, and we can quite understand that the apostles of the "glorious renaissance" should seize upon the idea.

All roads lead to Rome, and all lead from it. Mr. W. Barclay Squire tells us that in all probability it was from Italy that the earliest musical signals came, and spread over Europe by mercenaries, they were modified and altered by the different troops which adopted them. In fact, the names given to the different sounds long retained evidence of their Italian origin.[4] What the earliest signals were (in notation) we have no idea. The first English signals handed down to us date from the reign of Queen Mary, but they are *names* only. Trumpeters of "horse" were required to know—Saddle! Mount! Mess! March! Alarm! and Charge![5] Whilst the "foot" answered to the drum calls—March! Alarm! Approach! Assault!

'Grove, "Dictionary of Music."
'Fortescue, "History of the British Army."

Battle! Retreat! and Skirmish![6] We have no notation of English signals (I believe) earlier than the
eighteenth century. The Italians and French are more
fortunate. The former have trumpet signals recorded
in the collection of Girolamo Fantini (1636 or 1638),
and the latter were honoured by Mersenne (1635), who
included cavalry calls in his great work on music.
Mr. Squire has noticed several musical compositions of
an earlier period, such as Jannequin's "La Bataille,"
and his songs in Chemin's "Chansons" and Milano's
"La Battaglia," and suggests that they contain military signals, the comparison of which would probably
disclose points of interest between the French and
Italian signals. Now, I suggest that this might be
carried still further. England has several musical
compositions of a like character, so let the comparison
be extended to them. That interesting collection of
virginal music known as "My Ladye Nevell's Booke"
contains a section known as "Mr. Bird's Battel," composed by William Byrd towards the close of the sixteenth century. In this there are several pieces which
may be counted upon as embodying military signals.
Then there is a lute duet, "The Battle" (1616), and
another duet, "The Battle of Harlow" (1635?), and
an organ solo by Dr. Bull (1562-1628), "La Battaille."
Some of these may throw light on the question.

Although not practised as a necessary asset to military discipline, the march may be traced back to the

---

6 Grose, "Military Antiquities," 1801.

war-song of antiquity. As a strictly rhythmic piece of music for martial instruments, not only to stimulate and enliven troops, but to ensure a regular pace, it dates from the revival of the military art, about the late fifteenth century. Sir John Hawkins tells us in

Drummer.

Fig. 2.
DRUMMER (SEVENTEENTH CENTURY).

his "History of Music" (1776) that "the old English march of the foot was formerly in high estimation, as well abroad as with us; its characteristic in dignity and gravity, in which respect it differs greatly from the French, which, as it is given by Mersennus, is brisk and alert." Apropos of this, Sir John relates a *bon mot* of Sir Roger Williams, a soldier of the Elizabethan days, who, in answering the French Marshal Biron's remark that "the English march being beaten by the drum was slow, heavy and sluggish," said: "That may be true, but slow as it is, it has traversed your master's country from one end to the other."[7]

Marshal de Saxe pointed out in his "Reveries" that the sound of the drum was something more than a mere noise, and that the entire military art depended upon its various cadences. When pipes and fifes were made to accompany the drum, the precise beat of the latter fell into neglect. Markham clearly saw this when he said: "It is to the voice of the drum that the soldier should wholly attend, and not to the air of a whistle."[8] So serious did this inattention to the fundamental drumbeats become, that in 1610 a Royal warrant was issued for the better regulation of the old English march. Here is the warrant which appears in Walpole's "Catalogue of Royal and Noble Authors": "Whereas the ancient custome of nations hath ever bene to use one certaine and constant forme of March in the warres, whereby to be distinguished one from another. And the March of this our nation, so famous in all the honourable atchievements and glorious warres of this our kingdom in forraigne parts (being by the

---

[7] Hawkins, writing in 1776, says: "Notwithstanding the many late alterations in the discipline and exercise of our troops, and the introduction of fifes and other instruments into our martial music, it is said that the old English march is still in use with the foot."

[8] Markham, "Five Decades of Epistles of Warre," 1622.

approbation of strangers themselves confest and acknowledged the best of all marches) was through the negligence and carelessness of drummers, and by long discontinuance so altered and changed from the ancient gravity and majestie thereof, as it was in danger utterly to have bene lost and forgotten. It pleased our late deare brother prince Henry to revive and rectifie the same by ordayning an establishment of one certaine measure, which was beaten in his presence at Greenwich, anno 1610. In confirmation whereof wee are graciously pleased, at the instance and humble sute of our right trusty and right well-beloved cousin and counsellor Edward Viscount Wimbledon, to set down and ordaine this present establishment hereunder expressed. Willing and commanding all drummers within our kingdome of England and principalitie of Wales exactly and precisely to observe the same, as well in this our kingdome, as abroad in the service of any forraigne prince or state, without any addition or alteration whatsoever. To the end that so ancient, famous, and commendable a custome may be preserved as a patterne and precedent to all posterite," etc. This document also contains the following notation :

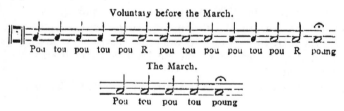

Voluntary before the March.

Pou tou pou tou pou R pou tou pou pou tou pou R poung

The March.

Pou tou pou tou poung

Subscribed "Arundell and Surrey. This is a true copy of the original, signed by his Majestie. Ed. Norgate, Windsor."

It was probably the neglect and carelessness of drummers that compelled the authorities to institute the office of drum major. Stainer and Barrett in their "Dictionary of Musical Terms," are of opinion that the office is not older than the reign of Charles II. This would appear true, since Turner in his "Pallas Armata" (1683) seems to have been unaware of the rank in our service. Yet we find him mentioned by quite half a dozen early seventeenth century writers,[9]

---

[9] Cruso (1632), Barry (1634), Hexham (1637), Ward (1639), Praissac (1639), and Venn (1672), all mention the drum major.

and the fact that Digges in his "Arithmetical Warlike Treatise" (1579) speaks of a "chief drummer," which in a later edition (1590) is altered to "drum major," enables us to fix a date even earlier. Although the rank appears on the establishment of regiments in the early seventeenth century, he seems to have dropped out during the Commonwealth. Afterwards, only the Foot Guards have him officially, and then the Royal Artillery. Marching regiments were not allowed a drum major (although they were rarely without one)[10] until 1810.[1] The special feature of the drum major is his "staff." When this was adopted I have no knowledge. Sometimes the drum major is described as the principal or solo drummer; but that he wielded the "staff" in some corps is evident from a "staff" preserved by the Honourable Artillery Company, bearing the date 1671.

---

[10] "Military Dictionary," 1778.
[1] James, "Military Companion," 1811.

CHAPTER III.

MILITARY MUSIC (1500-1700).

IT is not everyone that will assent to the dictum of the author of the "Garb of Old Gaul," that "the pipe breathes the true martial strain." Shakespeare makes a very "unkind cut" in "Much Ado About Nothing" when he says: "I'll devise thee brave punishment for him. Strike up 'pipers.'"

But Shakespeare was an Englishman, and it would be almost as reasonable to expect him to respond to a pibroch as for an Austrian to get excited over "Rule Britannia." Yet Englishmen had responded to a pibroch long before Shakespeare's day, for the pipe was highly popular in this country during the Middle Ages, and many a mile had our sturdy footmen trudged to its music. A large number of tunes to be found in Chappell's "Popular Music of the Olden Time" bear evidence of being of a bagpipe character.[2]

The pipe was a regular marching instrument with the Swedes, Germans and French. The latter, says

---

[1] Stainer and Barrett, "Dictionary of Musical Terms," 1898.

Kastner,[3] borrowed it from us. Stanihurst tells us that
with the Irish as well, the bagpipe was a warlike instrument, and according to Mr. Grattan-Flood[4] the well-
known picture of a piper by Dürer is a representative
from the "Land of Song." In Ireland, the break-up

Fig. 3.
PIPER (SIXTEENTH CENTURY).   BY ALBRECHT DÜRER.

of the Gaelic polity after the Cromwellian wars, put

---

[3] Kastner, "Manuel Général de Musique Militaire," 1848.
[4] Grattan-Flood, "History of Irish Music," 1906.

an end to the war pipes, and the last glimpse we have
of them, although in an alien clime, is with the Irish
Brigade at Fontenoy.

The bagpipe seems to have finally disappeared in
England about the same time, being gradually ousted
from its position as an accompaniment to the drum by
an instrument that remains to this day a favourite with
marching regiments. As late as 1674 a warrant is
issued for the appointment of one Peter Vanhausen,
to instruct a man in each company of the King's Regiment of Foot Guards the use of the pipe. But the
coup de grâce was not far distant. Sir James Turner
says in "Pallas Armata" (1683): "In some places a
piper is allowed to each company:[5] the *Germans* have
him, and I look upon their pipe as a warlike instrument. The bagpipe is good enough musick for them
who love it; but sure it is not so good as the Almain
Whistle (the fife). With us any captain may keep a
piper in his company, and maintain him too, for no
pay is allowed him, perhaps just as much as he
deserveth."

The introduction of the bagpipe into Scotland dates
only from the time of its disuse in England. Across
the Tweed they claim that the instrument was used at
Bannockburn. But it appears that the earliest mention
of the bagpipe as forming part of the military music

---

*In the infantry reorganised by Gustavus Adolphus, each
company was allotted three pipers and three drummers.—
Fortescue, "History of British Army."

of the Scots is at the battle of Balrinnes (1594)[6] since
when it has remained their special warlike instrument

What was this "Almain Whistle," which Shakespeare, whose eye and ear nothing escaped, referred to
as the "ear-piercing fife," that had so charmed the ears
of these military men? Nothing new to be sure
Simply the old idea of the Greeks, which the apostles
of the glorious renaissance had stumbled across
Machiavelli, who has been designated "the statesman
of the Renaissance," issued his "Art of War" in 1521,
which, like his histories and political science was cast in
the mould of classic antiquity.[7] It is not strange
therefore that Machiavelli should recommend the
ancient Greek method of employing flutes or fifes for
the better regulation of the stepping together of troops.
Foremost among those who adopted the idea were the
Swiss, whose famous soldiers led the way in all military
matters, and are even credited with its introduction
into military music[8]

As early as 1511, the fife is mentioned by Virdung
among the martial instruments of the Germans, and in
1534 it appears in the French service according to an
"Ordonnance" of Francis I, which allotted two fifes
and two tambourins to each company of a thousand
men.[9] That Rabelais makes the Andouille folk
attack Pantagruel to the sounds of "joyous fifes and

---

[6] Stainer and Barrett, "Dictionary of Musical Terms."
[7] Owen, "Skeptics of the Italian Renaissance," 1893.
[8] Grose, "Military Antiquities," 1801.
[9] "Memoirs de Du Bellay."

tambour," is some evidence that the instrument was
no novelty to the French soldier in 1535, when Rabelais's
great work was published. England soon followed
on the heels of France, and in the warlike muster of
the citizens of London in 1540, "droumes" and
"ffyffers" are well to the fore. So high did the fife's
popularity run in this country, that the demand very
soon outran the supply. Henry VIII, ever zealous in
military as in domestic affairs, sends specially all the
way to Vienna to obtain them,[10] whilst the State papers
contain not a few laments from commanding officers,
owing to the scarcity of these "wry-necked musicians,"
as Barnaby Rich calls them.[1] One writes that he can
only hire two of them, and these would only "sign on"
for a month at a time. Another says he could not get
any to serve under four men's wages, and even then
were "but easy players" and "very drunkards." Truly
these were troublesome times.

When one considers what was expected of them, it
is small wonder indeed that drummers and fifers were
hard to find. Listen to what one named Ralph Smith
(*tempore* Queen Mary) has to say.[2] "All captains must
have drums and fifes and men to use the same, who
shall be faithful, secret and ingenious, of able per-
sonage to use their instruments and office of sundry
languages; for oftentimes they be sent to parley with

" Fortescue, "History of the British Army," 1899.
'Rich, "Aphorisms," 1618.
'Grose, "Military Antiquities," 1801.

their enemies, to summon their forts or towns, to redeem and conduct prisoners, and divers other messages, which of necessity requireth language. If such drums and fifes should fortune to fall into the hands of the enemies, no gift nor force should cause them to dis- close any secrets that they know. They must oft practise their instruments, teach the company the sound of the march, alarm, approach, assault, battle, retreat, skirmish, or any other calling that of necessity should be known. They must be obedient to the command-ment of their captain and ensign, when as they shall command them to come, go or stand, or sound their retreat or other calling."

These drum and fife bands were but poor affairs of a very dull kind, says Kappey.[3] The side-drum was almost twice as large as the present instrument, and had no "snares," that rare contrivance that gives such a bright tone to the modern drum.[4] The fife was non-chromatic and its manipulation very rudimentary. What music they played we have but a faint idea. The earliest music for the fife to be found in an English work is in "Mars, His Triumph," by J. B, which is a description of an exercise performed at the Merchants Taylors' Hall in 1638 by the Artillery Company of London. The music was played by one fife and two drums, and accompanied the manual and firing exer-

---

Kappey, "Military Music."

In the "Syntagma Musicum" of Pretorius, 1619, the side drum is shown with "snares."

The Posture tune.

The Falling of Tune.

The Tune for the Motions.

Fig. 4.

MUSIC FOR THE DRUMS AND FIFES (FROM "MARS HIS
TRIUMPH," 1638.)

cises. The "Posture Tune" was for the firing exercise
—played once through for each posture. For the

manual exercise the "Falling Off Tune" was used—
once over for each rank. The "Tune for the Motions"
was played for all parade movements, such as facings,
doublings, etc.[5]

Fifer.

Fig. 5.

FIFER (SEVENTEENTH CENTURY).

Tabourot in his "Orchésographie" (1588) informs
those who perform on the fife, that they need simply
play according to their own pleasure, and it was sufficient so long as they kept time with the drum. As for
the drum, Markham—the author of "Five Decades of
Epistles of Warre" (1622), speaking of a certain book
of instruction in drumming, said he thought it an unnecessary study! Here were instructions which if fol-

⁵Cockle, "Bibliography of English Military Works," 1900.

6

lowed would scarcely have tended to improve these
drum and fife bands.   But neither Tabourot nor Markham could have meant all that they said, as the former
has left us several worthy specimens of drum and fife
music, whilst the latter devotes considerable space to
the use of drums and fifes, and bears witness, moreover, that he knew of "no more sweet and solemn
melody than that which the drum and flute afforded."

When the Commonwealth came, the English nation
entered into what Matthew Arnold called "the prison
of Puritanism," and all music other than psalms and
hymns was considered profane.   Ballad singers were
arrested on the highways, and throughout the length
and breadth of the land organs and other instruments
were destroyed wholesale.   Even the "waits" in the
large corporate towns were suppressed.   Although in
the army they could not very well dispense with such
important offices as the trumpeter and drummer, upon
whom they relied for their "sounds" and "signals,"
they were looked upon as a sort of necessary evil.[6]
That almost indispensable appendage to the march—
the fife, was banished from the service, whilst the drum
major, no small item in the musical display (Aye! there
was the rub) was even considered an unnecessary office.

When the King "enjoyed his own again," a splendid
cavalcade met him at St. George's Fields on the

' It is worth while noting that during this period the military musician is frequently paid less than the private soldier,
a most unusual thing.—See tables of pay, etc., in Fortescue's
"History of the British Army."

"glorious 29th of May, 1660, headed by the King's Life Guards, with their kettledrums and trumpets in front."[7] The first-named were the military instruments *par excellence* on the Continent, but quite new to us. Mr. W. Barclay Squire, who has given us a mine of information on this subject, is of the opinion that the use of these instruments for the cavalry came from - Germany, and quotes Fronsperger's "Kriegsbuch" (1566) and Tabourot's "Orchésographie" (1588) as evidence of their early use by German troops[8] There is, however, a still earlier record—that in 1542 our own King Henry VIII sent to Vienna for kettledrums that could be played on horseback "after the Hungarian manner," together with men that could make and play them skilfully.[9] That they were not then generally adopted in this country, we may gather from Nicholl's "Procession of James I."[10] Then we have the word of Sir James Turner (writing in 1671) who assures us that "they are not ordinary," and only used by *corps d'élite*, noblemen and general officers.[1] To fix the restoration as the date of their adoption by our army, would accord with Samuel Butler's mention of them in "Hudibras" (1663) among Magnano's "warlike engines."

---

[7] Cannon, "Historical Records of the Life Guards."

[8] Grove, "Dictionary of Music" (article, Military Sounds and Signals).

[9] Fortescue, "History of the British Army," 1899.

[10] Day, "Descriptive Catalogue of Musical Instruments," etc.

[1] Turner, "Pallas Armata," 1683.

In the German empire, the army was supplied with its musicians by a "guild" known as the "Royal Trumpeters and Army Kettledrummers," of ancient origin, and enjoying special privileges by Imperial decree. Anyone desiring to be initiated into the mysteries of trumpeting and drumming, had to be apprenticed to the guild, and could not practise his vocation until he had been made a "freeman." One curious privilege which it claimed was, that its members were exempt from military law, the guild holding itself responsible for the discipline of its members. With the Germans, kettledrums were only granted to *corps d'élite*, such as Life Guards and regiments whose colonels were nobles, excepting those that had captured their instruments on the battle-field.[2] This rule also found favour in France[3] where, says Kastner,[4] the introduction of the kettledrum preceded the reign of Louis XIV by a few years. In England, the "service" was furnished with its trumpeters and drummers by the sergeant-trumpeter and the drum-major-general of the royal household, who were empowered to "impress" the musicians they required for the king's army, when more peaceable methods had failed. Impressment seems to have been anything but

---

[1] Turner, "Pallas Armata," 1683.

[2] In later years this custom came in vogue in England and outside of the Life Guards, only the Royal Irish Dragoons and the King's Dragoons were allowed kettledrums, having captured them in battle.

[4] Kastner, "Manuel Général de Musique Militaire," 1848.

a pleasant occupation, for we find in the year 1637,
the sergeant-trumpeter appointed a "trumpeter-in-
ordinary" to impress one John Digges, when the latter
challenged him to fight and otherwise abused him !

In Grove's " Dictionary " it is stated that no mention
is made of the sergeant trumpeter of the Royal Household from the time of Benedict Browne (*temp*, Edward
VI) until 1641. This is not correct as there is the
appointment of Josiah Broome in 1626.

Fortescue notices a revival of the custom of impressment as late as 1705 and considers it an illegal stretch
of the royal prerogative[5], yet I find that even in 1781,
musicians were not safe from impressment, since the
Honourable Artillery Company in advertising for
drummers and fifers, promised immunity from impressment to those who would serve with them [6]

The reader has already noticed that trumpets and
kettledrums were the special property of the "upper
ten," a rule strictly adhered to in Germany. Even
here in "merrie England" anyone wishing to blow a
trumpet or beat a drum, other than the king's troops
had first to obtain a licence from the sergeant-trumpeter or the drum-major-general. Even with king's
troops, kettledrums were only granted to the royal
bodyguard. Thus we find that the Life Guards alone
had them. With this corps, each troop was allowed
four trumpeters and one kettledrummer, who held

[5] Fortescue, "History of the British Army."
[6] Raikes, "History of the Honourable Artillery Company."

good positions, having warrants of appointment
signed by the king, and paid like princes at five
shillings a day! Doubtless they were good musicians
at the price, but from a glance at their names in the
official records, they do not all appear to have been
cradled in Albion. On all occasions of state, the
trumpets and kettledrums of the Life Guards were in
attendance, and when their services were in demand
for dismounted purposes, we meet with the extra-
ordinary spectacle of the kettledrums carried on the
back of a man, and the drummer walking behind him.
It is believed to have been one of these trumpeter bands
of the Life Guards, which Cambert, the great French
composer, became bandmaster of, when he took refuge
in England in 1672. These musicians of the
Guards played on handsome silver trumpets, and
were clothed in the royal livery, of velvet coats,
trimmed with silk and silver lace, embroidered with
the royal cypher on the breast and back. The drums
and trumpets were also gaily decked with elaborate
banners, in fact the whole was much the same
as the state dress of the Household Cavalry bands
to-day.

When ordinary regiments of "horse" were permitted
to have kettledrums, one pair was allowed for the
colonel's troop with two trumpeters, each of the other
troops having to content itself with a couple of
trumpeters only. These when massed formed a band
of twelve to fourteen men, who played on the regula-

Fig. 6.

ARTILLERY KETTLEDRUMS AND CARRIAGE, 1700.

tion trumpet used for signalling[7] under the direction
of a trumpet-major.

Similar to the drummer and fifer, the trumpeter also
was expected to be a man of sundry accomplishments,
together with a comely figure, a good deportment and
the rest, but above all "a politic, discreet and cunning
person," says Elton.[8] In the "Souldier's Accidence"
(1635) it is laid down among the arms, accoutrements,
etc., of a trumpeter (which insists, by the way, that his
horse "shall be a good hackney with *gentleman-like*
furniture"), that he shall be provided with a sword
with the point broken! This was intended to show
that the trumpeter was distinctly a non-combatant, and
entitled to be respected as such. Military musicians
were held almost sacred in battle. At least, so it
appears from Markham's "Five Decades of Epistles
of Warre" (1622). He says of the drummer—he is to
be considered "rather a man of peace than of the sword,
and it is most dishonourable in any man wittingly and
out of knowledge to strike him or wound him."

Let us turn now to the music of the trumpeter bands.
That they played in parts, in "line" regiments, at any
rate, before the eighteenth century, is doubtful. Of
music for these bands, there is little or none extant; at
least in this country. No doubt most of the marches
and flourishes were learned by ear, for we are told that
these army trumpeters were not learned musicians, but

---

[7] Kappey, "Military Music."
[8] Elton, "Compleat Body of the Art Military," 1650.

were generally able to enliven the march of their corps with a few tunes.[9]

Even in France, up to the time of Rousseau,[10] their trumpeter bands played in unison.

Here is an example of this class of music taken from Kastner's "Manuel Général de Musique Militaire":

March for Trumpets.

(Seventeenth Century.)

'Kappey, "Military Music."

"Rousseau, "Musical Dictionary," 1768.

7

Perhaps the most novel example of military music was that of the Trains of Artillery, and as far as the writer can ascertain, was peculiar to the English service. The artillery employed kettledrums similar to those of the cavalry, but instead of being carried on horse-back, on either side of the drummer's saddle, they were mounted on a grand chariot, finely ornamented, and drawn by six white horses. They appear in the field of battle for the first time during the Irish Rebellion of 1689, and the custom lasted until 1759, when the artillery were divided into independent brigades. There is an interesting order issued during the Flanders Campaign, 1747, which directs the kettledrummer of the artillery "to mount the kettledrum carriage every night half-an-hour before the sunset, and beat until gun-firing."[1]

Here is an example of kettledrum music:[2]

March for Kettledrums. "Gardes du Roi de France." By Bablon.

(Seventeenth Century.)

---

[1] Farmer, "Memoirs, Royal Artillery Band," 1904.
[2] Kastner, "Manuel Général de Musique Militaire," 1848.

Kettledrummers as soloists seem very strange to us, yet listen to what Manesson Mallet says:[3]

"The kettledrum player should be a man of courage, preferring to perish in the fight, than allow himself and his drums to be captured. He should have a pleasing motion of the arm, an accurate ear, and take a delight in diverting his master by agreeable airs." Nowadays, "agreeable airs" for kettledrums in the orchestra are quite common, witness the solo for four drums in "Robert le Diable." I must confess, however, that Manesson Mallet's "agreeable airs" for a *pair* of drums must have been extremely "diverting"!

[3] Mallet, "Les Travaux de Mars, etc.," 1691.

CHAPTER IV.

HAUTBOYS.

THE "military band," as we understand the modern signification of the term, had its origin in the reign of Charles II. The tastes of this monarch were very much influenced by his residence in France, and on his accession to the English throne quite a new era begins for music in this country. French operas were played at court, and the services at the Chapel Royal were conducted similarly to those at Versailles. A court band of twenty-four violins was also instituted, in imitation of the "Vingt-Quartre Violons du Roi" of Louis XIV,[4] and even the military music of the French came under the covetous eyes of the "Merry Monarch." Their regimental bands com-

[4] It is worth mentioning here, that the term "band," which was applied to the French king's "violons," was also copied by Charles, at least, we may infer as much, since the word is used for the first time in relation to a body of musicians, in an order relating to the English "violins" in 1661.

44

prised of oboes, which appear to have been adopted
by them during the reign of the previous king.
Kastner, the historian of French military music, considers that they took the custom from the Germans.
Certain it is, that the oboe was not included among
the warlike instruments of the French when Tabourot
wrote in 1588.

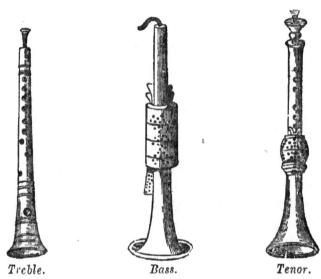

Treble.   Bass.   Tenor.

Fig. 7.

HAUTBOYS (17TH CENTURY).

With them, military music, apart from what was
really necessary for signalling, had no official sanction, and it was customary for commanding officers to
provide their own music if they required it. All this
was altered when Louis XIV became king. Lully, the
first composer in France, was entrusted by Louis with

the organization of his military bands, for which Lully
composed and arranged a large amount of music. As
I have already observed, these first military bands in
France consisted of oboes and drums, the authorities
allowing generally two oboes and two drums to each
company of infantry. Lully wrote for these in four
parts, *discant*, *alto*, *tenor* and *bass oboe* (or bassoon)
with two drum parts.[5] In the year 1705, the composer
Philidor, as the king's music librarian, collected an
enormous number of these military pieces which Lully
and himself had composed and arranged for the army,
many of which are still preserved at the Paris Conservatoire. Among them is the "Marche des Dragons
du Roi" for hautbois,[6] which is appended as an illustration of the music played by these bands.

March for Hautboys. "Dragons du Roi."

(Seventeenth Century.)

[5] Kappey, "Military Music."
[6] Kastner, "Manuel Général de Musique Militaire," 1848.

It is difficult to imagine how so delicate an instrument as the oboe, which Schubart in his "Æsthetic der Tonhurst" calls the "coquette of the orchestra," could have been of any service to the military. But we must remember that the oboe of that period was a very coarse thing compared to our modern instrument. It was non-chromatic, and played with a reed almost as large as that used with a present-day bassoon. Such an instrument was well adapted for military purposes, and we can readily accept the testimony of the learned Mersenne ("Harmonie Universelle," 1639), who said that it gave a tone louder than all other instruments, except the trumpet. Even in Mozart's day, it was so formidable that the composer of "Don Giovanni" remarked that it had such "impudence of tone," no other instrument could contend with it.

Oboes were introduced into the British service in the year 1678, when six of them were granted to the Horse Grenadiers, "a new sort of soldier," says

Evelyn, who served both mounted and dismounted. A few years later, when regiments of dragoons were raised, they were equipped similar to the Horse Grenadiers, and one oboe and two drums were allowed to each troop. The side drums used by them were much smaller than those of the foot regiments, and they were beaten in a different fashion.[7] The Foot Guards[8] and the marching regiments[9] then adopted the innovation, and the king evinced his interest by issuing a warrant (1684-5), "authorising the entertainment of twelve oboes in the king's regiments of Foot Guards in London, and that a fictitious name should be borne on the strength of each of the other companies quartered in the country with a view to granting these musicians higher pay."[10] This system of supporting bands by means of "non-effectives," as they were officially designated, afterwards became general throughout the service and lasted until the early years of the nineteenth century. In these "oboes" we have the real beginning of the military band in England.

During the first half of the eighteenth century, Germany led the way in matters of military music, and there can be no question that most of the European nations followed her example. The superiority of the Germans was so well established, that we read of Peter

[7] Kastner, "Manuel Général de Musique Militaire," 1848.
[8] Mackinnon, "History of the Coldstream Guards," 1833.
[9] "The Perfection of Military Discipline," 1690.
[10] Hamilton, "History of the Grenadier Guards," 1874.

the Great having his newly raised regimental bands fitted out by them, and even the King of Portugal had a supply of German trumpeters and kettledrummers. Rousseau in his "Musical Dictionary" of 1768, pays a high tribute to the fine bands of the Germans, and compares them to the wretched musical display of his own nation, who he says, had few military instruments and few military marches, most of which were *très malfaites*; although it seems that the inferiority of the military music of the French was a distinct gain to them, for their enemies (says Rousseau), hearing such bad music, thought they had recruits before them, and did not act with sufficient prudence, which caused them to be the victims of several engagements.

With the Germans, bands attached to regiments at the expense of the state, were, at first, a privilege granted to but few especially renowned regiments. But they were found to be such useful additions that in time every regiment obtained them. There was no fixed plan in the instrumentation of the bands, the arrangement of which rested with the colonel or bandmaster.[1] Since the beginning of the century, three new instruments had found their way into their bands, the bassoon, horn and clarinet. The bassoon was a great improvement upon the bass oboe or courtal which usually supplied the bass in the bands of oboes; in fact it is said that the name (originally *basson d'hautboy*) is derived from the early use to which it was put.[2]

---

[1] Kappey, "Military Music."
[2] *Ibid.*

8

The horn also supplied "a long felt want" as the advertising gentry say, in giving more stability to the inner parts, by sustaining important notes in the harmony. But it was the clarinet that had the greatest share in developing the resources of the military band. This instrument was the invention of a Nuremberg musician named Denner about 1690. "Its brilliant tone capable of every shade, from the softest to the loudest; its large compass, extending by the introduction of the smallest clarinets as well as by the bass clarinets, at once placed it in the rank of the leading instrument, and the oboe was pushed into the second place,"[3] and in many cases superseded it altogether. It first finds a place in the military bands, and for quite half a century remained with them entirely. Such an instrument must have been hailed with acclamation, especially when we consider its greater compass, safer manipulation (especially on the march) and a tone more adapted for outdoor work than the oboe. Kappey has preserved for us in his work on "Military Music," the score of a very tuneful military march, which includes a part for the clarinet, the earliest instance the writer has seen of its use. The date of the piece is 1720-30.

When we in England adopted the bassoon, horn and clarinet, it is difficult to say with any degree of certainty. Kastner says the French added these instruments to their bands during the reign of Louis

---

Kappey, Grove's "Dictionary" (article, Wind Band).

XV, and readily acknowledges that they copied the
Germans in this. Since a continental writer of the
period has said: "The English easily adopt innova-
tions from abroad, and complete their military bands
easily enough," we may assume that the English lost
little time in adopting these new instruments. Gras-
sineau in his "Musical Dictionary" (1740) does not
seem to have heard of the clarinet. As an orchestral
instrument it was first used in this country by Arne in
"Artaxerxes," 1762. The bassoon and horn were certainly in use with us before 1760.

It is most remarkable, that although this new
departure made for development by way of tone
colour, no advance resulted in augmentation. Regimental bands which invariably comprised from four to
six performers, might easily have been increased to
eight or ten with the advent of bassoons and horns
Instead of this, the bassoon takes the place of the bass
oboe or courtal, whilst a couple of horns oust a like
number of oboes. During the whole of the first half
of the eighteenth century, even the bands of the Foot
Guards numbered no more than six performers, two
oboes (or two clarinets), two horns and two bassoons
being the usual combination. There is an interesting
march for a band of this sort, in the "British Military
Journal" (1799).

How the ordinary regiments of infantry and cavalry
fared at this period, we know nothing definite, owing
to the scarcity of precise data; but we may take it for
granted that they would hardly be better equipped

than our regiments of guards. When bands of oboes first came into fashion at the close of the seventeenth century, the "line" regiments, both horse and foot, adopted them as readily as the guards. But the early years of the eighteenth century brought plenty of campaigning, which was scarcely propitious for the cultivation of bands. And, moreover, the State had always looked upon these institutions so purely as a matter of luxury, that no allowance was made for them, the entire support devolving upon the officers.

As there was no military school of music in those days for the training of army bandsmen, regiments were forced to engage musicians from civil life, and not being amenable to military discipline, these people were a constant source of anxiety to the authorities. On the Continent, this system of hiring bandsmen was evidently quite common, for we have a statement to that effect in some articles of capitulation of the Swedish garrison of Demmin in 1759, drawn up by the Prussians. The articles read: "The hautbois and musicians being paid by the officers shall be at liberty," and also that "the hautbois of Spen's Regiment may seek employment elsewhere, if it be true they were hired by the officers." Fortescue in his "History of the British Army" says that it was in 1749 that the first attempt was made to abolish the civilian bandsmen in our service.

The old system no doubt worked well from a musical point of view, for it was certainly the means of obtaining a better class of player, yet the luxury could only be indulged in by those corps whose officers were wealthy, and consequently the quality and condition of bands depended to a great extent upon the length of the officers' purses, and their musical tastes. That some took special care not to allow much latitude in this direction, witness an order dated 1731, for the Honourable Artillery Company, which provided that the music of the Grenadier Company should consist of "one curtail three hautboys *and no more*."[4]

One factor that specially deterred the progress of "bands" in England, was the revival of the "drums and fifes," which were adopted in 1748 after the Flanders campaign. This class of music soon came into great popularity with all foot regiments and even found its way into the cavalry.[5] A perusal of the soldiers' songs of the Dibdins will convey some idea of its vogue.[6]

Regiments of "horse" exhibited at first little inclination towards adopting the "band of music," for the simple reason that they thought them impracticable for mounted work, and appear to have been quite content with their trumpets and kettledrums, which were kept strictly on the lines of past centuries.[7]

---

[4] Raikes, "History of the Honourable Artillery Company."

[5] Hinde, "Discipline of the Light Horse," 1778

[6] Concerning introduction of the fife into the British service, both the Royal Artillery and the Foot Guards claim the honour. The question is dealt with fully in the author's "Memoirs of the Royal Artillery Band," 1904.

[7] Kappey, "Military Music."

Here and there, however, a band was adopted as we
are told in a work of 1760—the "Discipline of the
Light Horse" by Hinde.[8] But it served only for dismounted work, the trumpeter band alone being used
when mounted.[9] With regiments of dragoons matters
were on a different footing. They were available for
both mounted and dismounted duties, and had from
their inauguration employed bands of "hautboys,"
which appear to have undergone the usual development by the addition of bassoons and French horns.
By the middle of the eighteenth century, dragoons
became to be looked upon more as cavalry than
hitherto, and were drilled and accoutred as such.
Hence it was found that the side drum, as a signalling
instrument, was altogether out of place with them, and
the result that the trumpet was substituted. The
change was brought about (so 'tis said) by a Colonel
Dalrymple, who wrote in his "Military Essay" (1760)
concerning the merits of both instruments. However,
the order was issued in 1764[10] for the adoption of the
trumpet, although it was not put into effect until two
years later. Dragoons now having their trumpeters'
bands began to neglect their "bands of music,"
probably for the reason that the state provided for
their "trumpeter bands," as they did the "drums and

'This early edition of Hinde's book I have not seen, but I
quote from Fortescue's "History of the British Army."

'Hinde, "Discipline of the Light Horse," 1778.

" Grose, "Military Antiquities," 1801, says, "about the year
1759." Grove says the same.

fifes" for the infantry, whereas the "bands of music" were supported by a fund maintained mostly by the officers. Grose, the author of "Military Antiquities" (1786) tells a good story, in this connection, of the Duke of Marlborough, when he was General Church-hill. One day at a big review he was asked by the king, what had become of his "hautboys"[1] The general struck his hand on his breeches' pocket so as to make his money rattle, and answered: "Here they are please Your Majesty, don't you hear them?" The hero of Blenheim didn't believe in the "band fund," evidently!

---

[1] The title "band" or "band of music" was not generally adopted until the nineteenth century, although I find that Blackwell in his "Compendium of Military Discipline," 1726, speaks of the "band of music," and yet as late as 1834-5 the "Army Estimates" allow for "hautboys."

CHAPTER V.

A REVIVAL of interest in military bands in England follows on the heels of the peace of 1763, in accord with a general movement on the Continent. In Germany a special effort was made to establish the regimental band on a recognised model. This idea came from that great soldier who had held his own against "a world in arms"—Frederick the Great, King of Prussia. He was probably the first military commander, says the late Dr. Turpin, who realised the coming value to the soldier of the regimental band. He foresaw in a better cultivated system of military music, a new source of pride and delight for the soldier, and a new engine whereby military institutions would gain favour and popularity. Bands, as fixed by the order of Frederick the Great (1763), were to consist of: Two oboes, two clarinets, two horns and two bassoons, a combination, which was known on the Continent as *harmonie musik*, and a great favourite with composers. In France similar instruments were used by their guards' regiments from 1764, and somewhere about 1785-8 their infantry of the line adopted them.[2]   Austria raised bands for her army about 1769.

On the return of our army from the war on the Continent, several bands were brought over to this country, but the officers, says Mr. James. A. Browne (a first-rate authority in these matters)[3] "appears to have been at a loss to know what to do with them when the regiment went abroad again (most probably the performers refused to go), and . . . . they seem to have been handed over to militia battalions, as we frequently read of the bands of militia regiments, while the regulars had drums and fifes."[4] The best known of these bands that were "made in Germany," was that of the Royal Artillery, which was raised by those officers whose guns played such havoc with the enemy at Minden and Warberg. The "Articles of Agreement" (dated 1762) upon which this band was engaged, gives a fair idea of the constitution of a regimental band of the period.[5]

BAND OF MUSICK, ROYAL REGIMENT OF ARTILLERY, 1762.

I.   The band to consist of eight men, who must also be capable to play upon the violoncello, bass, violin and flute, as other common instruments.

---

[2] Kastner, "Manuel Général de Musique Militaire," 1848.

[3] For many years editor of the "British Musician," and later the "Orchestral Times."

[4] "British Musician," March, 1895.

[5] Farmer, "Memoirs of the Royal Artillery Band," 1904.

9

II   The regiment's musick must consist of two
trumpets, two French horns, two bassoons and four
hautbois or clarinetts;[6] these instruments to be provided by the regiment, but kept in repair by the head
musician.

III.   The musicians will be looked upon as actual
soldiers, and cannot leave the regiment without a
formal discharge.   The same must also behave them,
according to the articles of war.

IV.   The aforesaid musicians will be clothed by the
regiment.

V.   So long as the artillery remains in Germany
each musician to have ten dollars per month, but the
two French horns to have twelve dollars per month, out
of which they must provide their own bread; but
when they arrive in England, each musician to receive
one shilling, the two French horns one shilling and
twopence per day; this payment to commence at their
arrival in England.

VI.   The musicians shall be obliged to wait upon
the commanding officer so often as he shall desire to
have musick, without any hope of gratification, but if
they shall be desired to attend upon any other officer,
they are to have a ducat per night, but in England half
a guinea.

VII.   Should the aforesaid musicians be taken sick
they are to be attended by the surgeon of the regiment,

---

⁶ Ten instruments are here provided for eight men.—*Vide*
Clause I.

for which they are to allow fivepence farthing sterling monthly to be given out of their wages.

VIII. The two French horns will enter into pay, as soon as they sign their articles, the pay of the other six musicians, to commence as soon as they arrive at the corps.

IX. (In the handwriting of Colonel Phillips) Provided the musicians are not found to be good performers at their arrival they will be discharged, and at their own expense. This is meant to make the person who engages the musicians careful in his choice.

W. PHILLIPS,
Lieut.-Col. Comdt. of British Artillery.

Sundry instructions for "bands" are given in Simes's "Military Guide" (1772) and his "Military Course" (1777). Here are some of them: "The musicians must attend roll calling at all times when the regiment is on the march or under arms," and in action they are directed "to stay with their respective companies, and assist the wounded," practically the duties they perform to-day. Further, "they must be circumspect and exact in keeping their instruments of music in order, and that they practise three times a week." "The most skilful of the band ought to be appointed bandmaster," says our author. "To his care and inspection the others should be subjected"; and it was left to his discretion to "find out and practise the best adjudged pieces." For the guidance of commanding officers, in their "choice of music masters," the following hint was given them:

"They should be men whose regularity, sobriety, good conduct and honesty can most strictly be depended upon; that are most remarkably clean and neat in their dress; that have an approved ear and taste for music, and a good method of teaching; without speaking harshly to the youths, or hurrying them on too fast."

Another interesting sidelight on the requirements of bandmasters of the period, is an advertisement that appeared in the "Daily Advertiser" in 1774:

"WANTED, immediately, a person qualified as a Master Musician to a Military Band of Musick, who is a perfect master of the French Horn, and performs on other wind instruments, as great encouragement will be given. None need apply who is not a perfect master, and can be well recommended as a Person of great Sobriety and good character."

Observe, how all these people harp on "sobriety"! The "drunk as a fiddler" myth, was evidently still in full vigour at this date. In this connection, a reference to a most amusing article in James's "Military Dictionary" (1816) may not be out of place.

"It has often been asked why the dress of musicians, drummers and fifers, should be of so varied and motley a composition, making them appear more like harlequins and mountebanks than military appendages? The following anecdote will explain the reason as far

at least as it regards the British service: The musicians belonging to the guards formerly wore plain
blue coats, so that the instant they came off duty, and
frequently in the intervals between, they visited ale-
houses, etc., without changing their uniform, and thus
added considerably to its wear and tear. It will be
here remarked that the clothing of the musician falls
wholly upon the colonels of regiments; no allowance
being specially made for that article by the public. It
is probable that some general officer undertook to
prevent this abuse by obtaining permission from the
king to clothe the musicians, etc, in so fantastical a
manner that they would be ashamed to exhibit themselves at public houses, etc."

Needless to say, there is not a grain of truth in the
statement   So well informed a writer as James might
have known that it had been the custom from time
immemorial, to clothe musicians differently and on a
more lavish scale from the "rank and file." At the
period to which James refers, the general practice was
to dress musicians in the colour of the regimental
facings, in accordance with the Clothing Warrant of
1751. So that bands might be seen in a variety of
hues—red, blue, black, buff, white, orange, yellow and
green (the latter in seven different shades). But
revenons à nos moutons.

Although bands were now being raised everywhere,
the instrumentation was of the most meagre description. Nothing would persuade the authorities to shift
from the old *harmonie musik* combination. In the

"March of the Scottish Archers."

(Eighteenth Century.)

cavalry, six men sufficed for a band, two clarinets, two horns and two bassoons,[7] and in the infantry a band of eight performers (two oboes added to the preceding) was rarely exceeded. Here and there a flute, trumpet or bugle[8] were adopted, but usually at the expense of

[7] Hinde, "Discipline of the Light Horse," 1778.

[8] Mr. W. Barclay Squire in the new "Grove's Dictionary" tells us that bugle-horns were first mentioned in 1792. This is wrong. Grose ("Military Antiquities"—first edition) says that in the year 1761 there were some troops of Light Dragoons who used

some other instrument. Even an independent organisation like the Honourable Artillery Company could only boast of a band (1783) of four clarinets, two horns, one trumpet and two bassoons.[9] A good illustration of an arrangement for military bands of the period may be seen above [10]

The first notable additions to the military band were the serpent and trombone. The former was the natural bass of the ancient cornet family, which with this exception, had fallen into disuse. The bassoon had long been found insufficient to sustain the bass in the military band, and this now became the function of the serpent,[1] whilst the bassoon was pushed into its rightful sphere as a tenor instrument. The trombone was much later in making its appearance, not until the last decade of the century. Why this instrument, the true bass of the trumpet, should have lain idle so long, can hardly be explained, unless it was thought that the instrument would prove difficult to manipulate on the

---

horns like post-boys. There are also documents in existence which show that bugle-horns were used by the Grenadier Guards band in 1772 (Marr, "Music for the People"). In Hinde's "Discipline of the Light Horse" (1778) there is not only a list of the sounds allotted to the bugle-horn, but the instrument itself is delineated. Lastly, in the "Lives of the Lindsays," there is an account of an action at St. Lucia in 1778, where we are told that the "parley" was sounded on the bugle-horn instead of the drum, and the French not understanding the novelty, fired on a flag of truce.

[*] Raikes, "History of the Honourable Artillery Company."

["] Grieg, "Musical Educator."

['] Kastner, "Manuel Général de Musique Militaire," 1848.

march. It is more probable that the apparent neglect
proceeded from another cause. Once upon a time,
the trombone was "hedged" with a sort of divinity,
being confined to the use of church and king. But it
fell into disuse during the eighteenth century, and

Fig. 8.
SERPENT (c. 1780).

Burney tells us that for the Handel commemoration
of 1784, the only performers on the trombone to be
found in England, were in the King's Military Band.
No doubt, the adoption of the instrument by military
bands was the first step to its revival in this country.[2]

---

[2] It may be remarked here, that it is the opinion of two well-
known authorities (the Rev. F. W. Galpin and Mr. George
Case) that since its introduction into the military band, trombone playing has become coarse. Mr. Galpin thinks the per-

Kappey, in his "Grove's Dictionary" article on the "Wind-Band," is scarcely just to our military bands of this period. This is what he says: "England having in no way contributed to improve or even influence the progress of wind instrumental music, we have of necessity to pursue its course on the Continent, etc." Now this is not true. Kappey, being without data of the military music of the period (as he practically admits when he says: "It is difficult to trace' the introduction of military bands into the English service"), wrote the above to relieve himself of the necessity of explaining the *hiatus* in his historical survey.

In 1896, Breitkopf and Hartel published an elaborate edition of the "Music at the Prussian Court" ("Musik am Preussischen Hofe"), collected from the treasures of the Royal Library. Among them are several English marches and pieces for military bands. It appears that these were sent over to Germany, with other specimens of English music, including the works of Handel and J. C. Bach, on the occasion of the

---

version so serious that he recommends a return to the *diapason* tone, which was in vogue before the "military" got hold of the instrument. Now, I am not going to contest the statement any further than to call attention to that formidable passage for the trombone in the "Chorus of Furies" in Gluck's "Iphigenia in Tauride" (1779). This opera was written before the trombone came under the "doubtful influence" (*vide* Mr. Case) of the military, and yet who can imagine this "terrific scale" as Berlioz calls the passage in question, played *diapason*!

marriage of the Duke of York to Princess Frederica
of Prussia in 1791. Herr Georg Thouret, the editor
of the collection, makes some interesting remarks on
English military music of the period which I will
quote, together with others from Burney, Parke and
Pohl, as a foil to Kappey's depreciation.

"From the year 1750," says Thouret, "English military music made rapid and successful strides."
Twenty years later: "English military music had
no need to fear comparison with that of the Continent."
He also says that "the English military march . . . .
served as a model for Europe and made the graceful
6-8 time for marches popular."

The importance of English military bands of this
period may be argued from the fact that such eminent
musicians as J. C. Bach, William Crotch, William
Shield, Renaigle, Dibdin, K. F. Horn and Malchair,
of Oxford, wrote for them.

Rousseau had paid a great compliment to the bands
of the Germans, and indeed it was the general impression that military music had reached its highest
development with them. Yet, that our English bands
were as good as anything on the Continent, we have it
on the authority of no less a person than the eminent
musical historian, Burney. In his "Present State of
Music in Germany," he writes under Mannheim (1772):
"The first music I heard was military. I lodged on
the Place d'Armes, or parade; the retraite had only
drums and fifes; and in the morning there was nothing
worth listening to. If I had had an inclination to

describe in a pompous manner merely the effects of wind instruments in martial music, there had been no occasion to quit London; for at St James's, and in the park, every morning, we have now an excellent band; and hitherto, as I had not seen more soldier-like men in any service than our own, so the music and musicians of other places, exceeding ours in nothing but the number and variety of the instruments; our military music, at present, must seem to have made great and hasty strides towards perfection, to all such as, like myself, remember, for upwards of twenty years, no other composition made use of in our foot guards than the march in 'Scipio,' and in our marching regiments, nothing but side drums."

Frederick Nicolai (1733-1811), another musical *littérateur* who visited Vienna in 1781, speaks in terms of high praise of a military band which consisted of two shawns (? oboes), two clarinets, two horns, one trumpet, two bassoons and a side and bass drum, and expresses astonishment at Burney who heard it while he was collecting materials for his great history, yet did not think it worthy of mention.[3] After reading Burney's encomium of our bands, we can quite understand why he failed to notice the Viennese band.

Burney's reference to the march in "Scipio," is extremely interesting, since it partly confirms the tradition which Rockstro mentions in his "Life of Handel," that the well-known strains which open the first act of

---

Kappey, "Military Music."

opera, was specially composed by Handel as a parade
slow march for the Grenadier Guards before it was
introduced into "Scipio." This opera was composed
in 1726, and we may reasonably infer (accepting the
truth of the story) that the band of the Grenadier
Guards at this date was certainly no "hole and
corner" affair to attract the attention of Handel. The
stately old march is still played by this band under
the title of the "Royal Guards March." While speaking of marches, it may be of interest to mention a
march which Samuel Wesley composed when a boy,
specially for one of the guards' bands, part of which
was published for pianoforte in the "Musical Times,"
March, 1907. What the original arrangement was is
not stated. It was probably the march composed in
1777 for horns, oboes, bassoons and serpent mentioned
in the list of his works.[4]

Of the development of the bands of the foot guards,
we have an account in the "Musical Memoirs" of
W. T. Parke, one of the leading oboe players in
London at the close of the eighteenth century. The
author says: "The bands of the three Regiments of
Guards consisted in 1783 of only eight performers, two
oboes, two clarinets, two horns and two bassoons. They
were excellent performers on their instruments, and
hired by the month, being well paid. They were not
attested, and only played from the parade at the
Horse Guards to St. James's Palace while the King's

' Grove, "Dictionary of Music," etc.

Guard was mounted, and back again from there to the Horse Guards. Lord Cathcart, an officer of the Coldstreams, desired the band to play during an aquatic excursion to Greenwich. This the musicians deemed incompatible with their respectable musical engagements and they declined to do it The officers, who had to subscribe the pay of the band, became desirous of having a band which they could command on all occasions, and a letter to that effect was written to the Duke of York, colonel-in-chief of the regiment. The duke being at that time in Hanover, consented to the wish of his officers, and, with the approval of the king, a band of a much larger number than hitherto employed, and entirely composed of Germans, was sent over. It consisted of twenty-four members, and included clarinets, horns, oboes, bassoons, trumpets, trombones and serpents, whilst three black men were employed to beat the tambourine and carry a crescent."

Pohl, in his "Mozart and Haydn in London," gives an account similar to the above, adding that this Guards' band reached such a state of perfection as "to attract the public to St. James's Park," where it performed daily, and moreover gave the idea to the Prince of Wales (afterwards George IV) of forming his famous court military band.

Parke and Pohl are wrong, however, in one particular. The regimental records show that this first band of attested soldiers for the Coldstreams was formed in 1785, when twelve (*not* twenty-four) musicians were enlisted in Hanover by the Duke of York, one

of their number, Christopher Frederick Eley, being
appointed bandmaster with the high-sounding title of
"music-major." The performers comprised four
clarinets, two oboes, one trumpet, two horns, two
bassoons and one serpent. The trombones and the
three black men with their "Turkish music" mentioned
by Parke and Pohl were later additions. It was the
adoption of the latter which resulted in a complete
alteration in the character of military bands, and was
the means of giving it a defined position in the realms
of music.

CHAPTER VI.

TURKISH MUSIC.

A RATHER prominent influence upon the construction of the military bands of Europe, says Mr. Kappey,[5] was exercised by those of the Janissaries, the powerful soldiers of the Turkish empire. Their bands usually comprised three small and two large oboes, and one or more fifes, all of a very shrill character which were shrieked in unison, to the accompaniment of three kettledrums—one large and two small, three or more tenor drums and one big bass drum whilst three pairs of cymbals and a couple of triangles were thrown in to lend additional colour. No wonder their enemies were vanquished, for this noise must have been simply irresistible. The noise notwithstanding, neighbouring princes soon became enamoured —at any rate with their appearance (as they were usually dressed in the most extravagant eastern style),

---

[5] Kappey, "Military Music."

71

and the King of Poland obtains from the Sultan one
of these bands in "full rig." In a very short time the
"Turkish music" contagion takes a hold of most
European armies. The foundation of military bands
in the Austro-Hungarian is said to date from 1741,
when the Chevalier von der Trenck marched into
Vienna at the head of his troops, preceded by a
Turkish band. About the same time it finds its way
into the *corps d'élite* of France, and Marshal de Saxe
employs it in his Uhlans, during the war of 1741. This
famous soldier had great faith in the value of the
military band, and in his "Réveries" he gives as one
reason the Romans were generally victorious, that they
were made to march in time. "This," he says, "is the
perfect secret. . . . . It is the reason of the institution
of marches and the beating of the drum." Even that
mighty statesman and general, Frederick the Great,
could not rest until he had sampled this "Turkish
music," and so pleased was he with the imposing
appearance of these orientals and their "tools" as
Wagner would say, that he introduced percussion instruments into all his regimental bands, engaging
turbaned and bedizened negroes to manipulate them.

Although this was "all the rage" on the Continent
for quite half a century, England showed not the
slightest inclination to add to the time-honoured *harmonie musik* combination by adopting it. Perhaps we
ought to credit her with good sense. Yet Handel had
the temerity to advise Gluck, who had failed to satisfy
a London audience with the opera, "La Caduta di'

Giganti," that his music was too good for them. "If
you want to work for the English," said Handel, "you
must give them something tumultuous, like the rattle
of drum-sticks or a drum."[6]   As to the exact date when
England succumbed to the "Turkish music" craze I
am not quite certain. Grove says between the years 1805
and 1808, but that is not correct.   The Royal Artillery
band had it as early as 1786.[7]   There is an interesting
reference to its introduction into the Guards' bands in
Mrs. Pappendiek's chatty volumes, " Court and Private
Life in the Time of Queen Charlotte."   Under the year
1788 (November) she says : " One circumstance greatly
disturbed and vexed the King, and it is feared brought
forward his direful malady to a more violent crisis,
was the return of the Duke of York from Hanover,
without permission, and the unceasing endeavours of
His Royal Highness to persuade the King to allow
him to introduce into the Guards' bands the Turkish
musical instruments, with the ornamental tails,
crescents, etc."

Black men were, however, no novelty in our service,
for in an interesting record of the Twenty-ninth Regiment by Major Everard, there are many particulars
relative to the black drummers of that corps, who were
first introduced in 1759.[8]   They appear to have had
even an earlier existence, as Scott introduces these

[6] Newman, " Gluck and the Opera," 1895.
[7] Farmer, " Memoirs of the Royal Artillery Band," 1904.
[8] Everard, "History of Thos. Farrington's Regiment," 1891.

"sable" musicians into "Old Mortality," and I have
seen a negro kettledrummer in a battle picture, "Blenheim, August 18, 1704," by R. Caton Woodville. A
negro trumpeter in state dress, of the Royal Horse
Guards (1742) is also shown in R. Simkin's "Our
Armies."

We may rest assured that our marching regiments
soon recognised the enormous value of this "Turkish
music," for the better regulation of the march. This
was always a question of the highest importance in our
service, and at the beginning of the nineteenth century,
stringent regulations were issued to general officers of
districts to report half-yearly whether bands in their
command could "play in correct time." For the
guidance of drum-majors and others it was ordered
that "they should be attentive not to deviate in the
most trifling degree from the time which will allow,
within the minute, the exact number of steps prescribed by H.M. regulations."[9] To acquire the precise
step the drum-major was compelled to practise his
musicians to the "plummet,"[10] whilst on the march he
ensured a regular pace by a systematic motion of his
staff or baton, which by the regulations he was required
to turn "with an easy air one round, so as to keep time,
and plant it at every fourth pace."[1]

Such excellent pace-makers as the bass drum and

---

[9] "Regulations for the Army," 1811.
[10] "Regulations for the Army," 1811.
[1] James's "Military Companion," 1805.

cymbals would therefore be hailed with acclamation by the marching regiments, and were taken up immediately. Besides these, there was the triangle, tambourine,[2] kettledrum and an instrument known to the "tommies" as the "Jingling Johnnie" or more politely as the *chapeau chinois*, all of which were included under the heading of "Turkish music." The "Jingling Johnnie" has long since passed away, and an illustration is appended on that account. It was simply a pole surmounted by several crescents from which depended innumerable small bells. The shaking of its "sonorous locks," as Berlioz says, at regular intervals, gave much brilliancy to marching music.[3]

The black men who played these instruments were dressed in most elaborate uniforms, with gorgeous slashed tunics and high feathered turbans of great splendour.[4] It was part of their business to perform all sorts of contortions and evolutions whilst playing their instruments. One writer says:[5] "I have often

---

'These were very large. Colonel Shaw-Hellier exhibited one at the Worshipful Company of Musicians' Exhibition, dated *circa* 1750 (? later).

'It fell into disuse about sixty or seventy years ago. The idea survives in the modern glockenspiel or "chimes," an instrument constructed of vibrating bars of steel, played with a metal "striker." Among other survivals of the "blacks," I may mention the tiger or leopard skin which adorns the big drummer nowadays, and the display which drummers make with their sticks.

'Everard, "History of Thos. Farrington's Regiment," 1891.

'"British Bandsmen," August, 1890.

Fig. 9.

JINGLING JOHNNIE.

heard old soldiers of that period talk of the antics these negroes were so fond of displaying while on the march, such as throwing up a bass drum-stick into the air after the beat, and catching it with the other hand in time for the next; shaking the 'Jingling Johnnie' under their arms, over their heads, and even under their legs, and clashing the cymbals at every point they could reach."

But matters were really overdone in this particular, and regiments returning from West Indian service were the objects of envy in proportion to the number of "blacks" they could muster in the ranks of their bands. A writer in the "Quarterly Musical Register" for 1812, willingly allows that although a great number of excellent performers are to be found in the military bands, he complains that their music "is so often drowned by the drumming, and other *noise*, with which it is too frequently accompanied." Some bands actually had quite one third of their members performing upon instruments of percussion. They had the good sense, however, to introduce in time a further variety of wind instruments to reduce this preponderance of noise. But this I will deal with in another chapter.

A word in conclusion about the "blacks." They remained a feature of our bands until the accession of Queen Victoria, and in less than ten years from then scarcely any regiments had one on their establishment. Possibly the last in the cavalry was the black trumpet-major of the Fourth Light Dragoons, who served as

late as 1842.[6]   The Twenty-ninth Foot, who had made
a specialty of their "blacks," parted with their last man
in 1843.[7]   The Second Life Guards employed three
black trombone players until just before the Crimean
War, and the Coldstream and Scots Guards had one
man each at the same time. John Baptist was the
name of the "coloured" gentleman of the Scots, but
alas! he was no "forerunner"; he was the last of his
profession, and very soon, he too had "gone where de
good niggers go."

[6] Marr, "Music and Musicians," etc., 1887.
[7] Everard, "History of Thos. Farrington's Regiment," 1891.

CHAPTER VII.

THE INFLUENCE OF THE FRENCH REVOLUTION.

FROM the military spirit aroused by the first French republic, and more especially through the inordinate elevation of military life by the great Napoleon, came a fresh impulse to military music, the development of which was destined to outstrip in some respects, the progress then taking place in Prussia. When the opera house and the fashionable concerts of the aristocracy closed their doors for lack of patrons, the musicians transferred their services to the bands organised by the people. For the grand fêtes of the revolution, wind bands of enormous proportions were organised, and the first composers in the land wrote for them. Foremost amongst the bands which took part in these great public ceremonials, was that of the National Guard. It was formed at the outbreak of the revolution by a Captain Sarrette, who gathered together forty-five able military bandsmen for this purpose. The strength was then raised to seventy, and no less a person than Gossec, the most

important French composer in the latter half of the
eighteenth century[8] was appointed bandmaster, with
Catel as his assistant. They wrote a vast amount of
music for military bands, including symphonies. After
three years this band was dissolved by the Convention,
but Sarrette managed to keep his players together, and
eventually formed a free music school, in which the
members of the band were appointed teachers. When
the military spirit was abroad once again, it was
Sarrette's school that provided regimental bands for all
the *corps d'armée* of France, which led the Convention
to bestow upon the school the title of "Institut National
de Musique." In 1795, this was amalgamated with the
"Ecole du Chant et du Declamation," under the decree
of the government as the "Conservatoire de Musique,"
Sarrette being appointed director, the first of that
brilliant line which includes Cherubini, Auber and
Ambroise Thomas. Thus the world-renowned Paris
Conservatoire had its origin in the ranks of military
music.

Under Napoleon, military bands made enormous
strides, not only in matter of numbers, but in executive
capacity. In 1802 however, for reasons of economy,
he suppressed bands in cavalry regiments, and is said
to have remarked that the cavalry bandsmen were
monopolising horses and equipment with which he
could furnish four regiments. When financial pros-
pects for the army were brighter, the cavalry had their

'Naumann, "History of Music."

bands restored. They were instrumented thus: Sixteen trumpets, six horns and three trombones, but kettledrums were only allowed to the guards, cuirassiers and carbiniers.[9]

In the regiments of infantry, bands comprised:

1 Flute (Small).	2 Cymbals.	2 Side Drums.
1 Clarinet, F.	2 Trumpets.	1 Bass Drum.
16 Clarinets, C."	1 Bass Trumpet	1 Tenor Drum
4 Bassoons.	(Buccin).	2 "Jingling John-
2 Serpents.	4 Horns.	nies."
1 Triangle.	3 Trombones.	Total, 43.

These fine bands of the Napoleonic armies, says Kappey, were considered the finest in existence, hence the great influence they exercised upon the improvement of those of other nations, with whom the conqueror came in contact. "Composers for the first time got a conception of the capabilities of this hitherto despised branch of musical art; open air music was lifted into a superior position." How this great movement influenced our bands in England we shall see presently.

It has been said that the best military bands in this country a century ago were those attached to the militia and volunteers, which since their reorganisation during the American War, had become a very popular branch of the service In Ireland too,

---

[9] Napoleon instituted a school for cavalry trumpeters at Versailles which existed from 1805 to 1811.

[10] Clarinets in F and C were employed universally in military bands at this period. Note Beethoven's works for same, and Mendelssohn's Overture in C. In France, the B flat (and the E flat?) came into use in 1814, and were made compulsory in 1825.

says Mr. Grattan Flood, the era of volunteers (1774-84) was marked by band music, and almost every corps had a wind band. The superiority of these bands may be easily accounted for. First, the musicians were engaged, not enlisted as soldiers. Secondly, the colonels and officers were generally wealthy noblemen and gentlemen resident in the counties, and well able to maintain these bands. The bandmasters were invariably eminent local musicians.

The famous astronomer, Sir William Herschell (1738-1822) was at one time bandmaster of the Durham Militia (*circa* 1759). John Köhler, the instrument maker, was bandmaster of the Lancashire Volunteers some time prior to 1780. The well-known John Parry (1776-1851), composer and critic, was bandmaster of the Denbigh Militia (1797-1807). Samuel Mather (1783-1824), the founder of musical festivals in Yorkshire, and a fine organist, was bandmaster of the Sheffield Volunteers (1805). Johann Logier (1777-1846), the inventor of the "chiroplast," was bandmaster of the Kilkenny Militia (1807).

Among these bands of the auxiliary forces there were some curious combinations. For instance, the R.E. Middlesex Militia, about 1776, had a band of "Pandean reeds," for which the bandmaster, H. Eberhardt, published a tutor, the preface of which contains instructions of such an original character that they are worth reproducing. First we are told that the "Pandean pipes are instruments now generally used in regimental bands and much approved of in the King's

Guards." Then we have the following directions for their use :

"There are four pipes commonly used, viz.: First, second, Tenor and Bass : the first thing to be acquired on this instrument is to sound every note clear and distinct, which is done by placing the Instrument against the Lips in a direct line, and blowing into each pipe, which is done without any difficulty, giving each Note a distinct articulation, except in Bars of Music consisting of running passages which are executed very rapid, passing clear and distinct from Pipe to pipe, tipping the first note of every passage. The key of this instrument is generally in the key of D Major, with two sharps, consequently the other Instruments which assist are put in corresponding keys. The B Fifes or Flutes, serve as an excellent support to the reeds, the Music for which in order to play with them are transposed (provided the reeds are in the Key of D) into the key of G. The thirds are produced in a manner surprising and with great effect by pressing the Lips against the centre Pipe of two, and blowing at each outside Pipe. Observe, when an accidental Note occurs as G sharp or C Natural, it must be taken by the Flutes or Fifes, accompanying the Pipes, and all the small notes, where there are two, must be taken by such instruments."

Then there is a record of another band, which occurs in a letter written in 1793 by Mr. W J. Mattham, an innkeeper at Lavenham, Suffolk, which says :

"We have had four (?) companies of the West

Middlesex Militia quartered upon us for three days, consisting of three officers and forty-nine men, who had the best band I ever heard—'tis worth mentioning for those who are lovers of superior music. It consisted of five clarinets, two French horns, one bugle horn, one trumpet, two bassoons, one bass drum, two triangles (the latter played by boys about nine years old); and the clash-pans by a real *blackamoor*, a very active man, who walked between the two mulattos, which had a very grand appearance indeed."

Whatever was the state of music in England at the close of the eighteenth century, the military bands, at any rate, compared favourably with those on the Continent. We have already seen that Burney had passed a similar opinion in 1777, and from a glance at the following tables it will be evident that the same excellence was maintained :

ENGLAND. (1794.) GRENADIER GUARDS.	FRANCE. (1795.)[1] CORPS D'ELITE.	PRUSSIA AND AUSTRIA. (1800.) LINE REGIMENTS.
1 Flute.	1 Flute.	2 Flutes.
6 Clarinets.	6 Clarinets.	2 to 4 Clarinets.
3 Bassoons.	3 Bassoons.	2 Oboes.
2 Serpents.	1 Serpent.	2 Bassoons.
1 Trumpet.	1 Trumpet.	2 Trumpets.
3 Horns.	2 Horns.	2 Trombones.
Drums, etc.	2 Drums, etc.	1 Serpent or Contra Bassoon.
		4 Drums, etc.

The influence of the mighty wind instrumental

---

[1] This, according to Kastner. Fétis gives the following as the composition of French regimental bands under the Revolution : One piccolo, two horns, four clarinets, two hautbois, two bassoons, three drums, etc.

combinations of Napoleon's armies, then came to be felt, and progress was, as the French say, "in the air." As an illustration of the rapid developments which our bands were making, we may take the band of the Royal Artillery. Until 1792 this organisation only numbered *eight* musicians. In this year *nine* are allowed, and two years later the strength is increased to ten. In 1802 an augmentation is made to *twenty-one*, and in 1812 the band numbers *thirty-five* exclusive of three black drummers. Such developments as these would scarcely pass unnoticed, and so we find in the "Quarterly Musical Register" for 1812 (No. 3) there is "a retrospect of the state of music in Great Britain since the year 1789," and the "military band" is included in the survey. We are told that:

"The *military bands of music* have been much enlarged, and the serpent, trombone and the German flute, as well as the different kinds of smaller flutes, have been introduced in them, which formerly were not generally used. England therefore has at present a great number of excellent performers on the different wind instruments."

Towards the close of the eighteenth century our cavalry regiments began to perceive that something might be done in the way of improving their music for mounted purposes. Although cavalry regiments had generally adopted bands for dismounted duties, the trumpets and kettledrums were all they could boast of when "boot and saddle" sounded. The first step towards extending the scope of the trumpeter bands, was the recognition of the French horn, which was found useful in sounding the more elaborate signals, the "retreat" for instance. Combined with the trumpet, some "showy" flourishes could be obtained, and the authorities were not slow to observe the excellent results. All that was now required was a "bass," and so the natural complement to the trumpet family was requisitioned—the trombone. Then another instrument takes a place in mounted bands—the serpentcleide (a portable serpent), which in later years, when constructed in brass was known as the "bass horn." In Maclise's picture of the meeting of Wellington and Blücher at "La Belle Alliance," there is depicted a mounted band of a Prussian hussar regiment which consists of trumpets, French horns and bass horns.

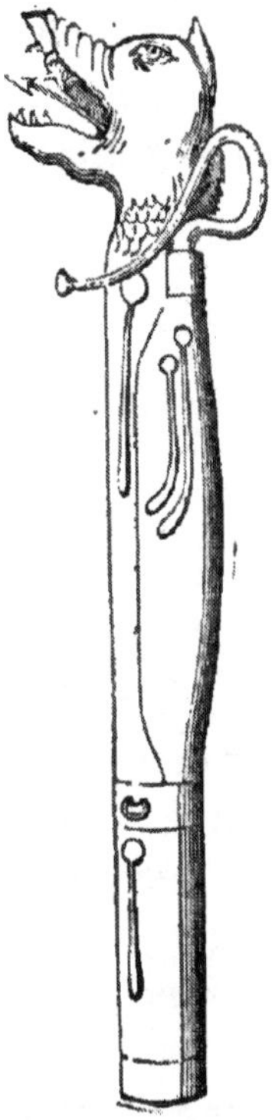

Fig. 10.
SERPENTCLEIDE.

The date when mounted bands generally came into vogue, cannot be located with certainty. The last decade of the eighteenth century would perhaps be a fair guess. At all events, our two regiments of Life Guards had them in 1795.

In these days there were no such things as "valves" in brass instruments, and their scale was therefore imperfect. So we can understand how limited the efforts of these brass bands were, being restricted

to the harmonics of their instruments. Some little
variety had been obtained by having trumpets and
horns pitched in various keys, but to little purpose,
from a point of progress. There had been the application of the slide to the trumpet, after the manner of
the trombone, yet it appears to have been neglected.

Fig. 11.
KEY-BUGLE.

Then came the invention of a "valve," although not as
we understand it at present, by an Irishman named
Clagget. To this also little attention was paid. There
is, however, a record that the first circular bass tuba
with rotary action valves used in this country, was
made for the Second Life Guards in 1809,[2] which was
probably on Clagget's system.

The first really successful attempt at giving a complete scale to brass instruments was the invention of
the key-bugle. This was brought out by James Halliday, bandmaster of the Cavan Militia, who registered
his patent in 1810.[3] The Duke of Kent heard Halliday

[2] Rose, "Talks with Bandsmen."

[3] Riemann, in his "Dictionary of Music," says the key-bugle
dates from 1820-35, which is incorrect.

perform on the instrument at Dublin, and was so struck with the innovation that he encouraged its adoption by our regimental bands. Halliday out of compliment to his patron called the instrument the Royal Kent Bugle, and not only did it become the mainstay of our bands, but also found its way into the orchestra. The excellent performances of Distin, the solo bugle player in the Grenadier Guards band, led Sir Henry Bishop to assign it a solo in his overture to "Guy Mannering" (1816).

From the idea of the key-bugle, an instrument which afterwards became a valuable adjunct to both the military band and orchestra, was evolved, viz, the ophicleide. It was simply a bass key-bugle, being an octave lower than that instrument. It is recorded[*] that at the Battle of Waterloo the ophicleide was used by both the English and Belgian armies, and Grove says that it seems agreed on all hands that the French were made acquainted with the instrument during the occupation of Paris by the allies in 1815.

This brings us to the war with France, which I must not forget to mention in connection with bands. During the campaign in the Peninsular the line regiments had their bands with them at "the front." Although it was the regulation, or at least the custom to send bands to the rear whenever a battle was imminent, yet we frequently read of them in the "fighting line." At Busaco, our soldiers, weary and

---

* Rose, "Talks with Bandsmen."

starving, were hard pressed by the French, and victory seemed questionable. The Duke of Wellington at once sent forward the bands to play the national

anthem, and instantly the men seemed to fight with fresh vigour. The battle was won. An officer who was present, subsequently wrote: "I saw one company waver, but a non-commissioned officer shouted that as long as that music lasted every man should fight, and he would put a bullet into the first person who exhibited signs of cowardice." At Talavera, two bands were entrenched in a ravine out of the way of the flying bullets, and with stirring music goaded on their comrades. At Salamanca the Thirty-second were fortunate to recapture the big drum which their band lost during the retreat to Corunna.

An interesting account of the band of the Forty-eighth Regiment during this campaign may be found in Cobbold's "Mary Ann Wellington." From this work we find that the Forty-eighth raised their band in 1798. The band

Fig. 12.

OPHICLEIDE.

of this regiment in the war, consisted of thirteen men, and the bandmaster and drum major. The exploits of the latter fill quite half of Cobbold's book.

13

All this campaigning would scarcely leave regimental bands in good form, and it is feared that they earned an experience somewhat similar to that afterwards obtained in the Crimea. An old Peninsular officer said[5] that he never felt so ashamed of our meanness and neglect of military prestige, as when he marched into Paris in 1814, and heard the fine bands of other nationalities, compared to the meagre and scanty musical display of the British troops.

Then came Waterloo. Bands have been mentioned[6] as having taken part in the great battle, but there is no mention of them in any of the accounts of that event, or in any regimental record.[7] After the battle bands appear much in evidence. It is recorded[8] that our regiments had their bands when they made their entrance into Paris, and on that occasion played a

---

[5] "British Bandsmen," April, 1888.

[6] Rose, "Talks with Bandsmen."

[7] At the Royal Military Exhibition (1890), Messrs. J. and R. Glen, of Edinburgh, exhibited a bassoon "believed to have been used" by the Forty-second Highlanders during the 1815 campaign. There is also a bass drum belonging to Seventh Hussars, said to have been picked up on the battlefield of Waterloo ("Worshipful Company of Musicians' Exhibition Catalogue," 1904). Against the use of the latter at the battle of Waterloo one writer has urged, that as the Seventh Hussars were mounted at the battle, a bass drum would have been no use to a mounted band. This is quite an error. Mounted bands of the period carried the bass drum on horseback (see Kastner), and even in recent years a similar custom was in vogue in Austria.

[8] "Dictionary of Musicians," 1825.

march based on the patriotic song, "The Glorious Sixth of May."

Our regiments of foot guards, not to be outdone by the Germans and Austrians who formed part of the allied army, and were well provided with bands, gave instructions for their bands, left behind in London, to proceed to France to join their regiments which were to form part of the army of occupation. So the bands of the First Grenadier Guards, Coldstream Guards and Scots Fusilier Guards were stationed in Paris for the period of about six months. During a grand review which took place before the Grand Duke Constantine of Russia, the Marquis of Wellington, and other distinguished officers of the allies, the band of the Grenadier Guards attracted considerable attention, and the Grand Duke was very much impressed by a member of the band who played the key-bugle. This instrument was a great novelty at the time, and the performers were usually placed for "show" on the wings of the front rank.[9] The Grand Duke was curious to learn something about the new instrument, and the band was ordered to cease playing, the performer, who was the famous John Distin, being commanded to appear before His Highness. The Duke carried on an animated conversation upon the merits of the key-bugle, and Distin was asked to obtain an instrument for him to take back to Russia. Halary (not Halévy, as Distin's son,

---

' Hence no doubt the origin of the German name for a similar instrument the Flügel horn.

Theodore, relates) the famous Paris instrument maker was commissioned to make a replica of Distin's instrument, which was eventually presented to the Duke. It may be added that Distin was handsomely rewarded for his pains. Two years afterwards Halary patented his key-bugle family of three—the clavitube (a key-bugle), quintitube (an alto ophicleide) and the ophicleide, which were adopted by the French army. This is the only reference I have seen to our Guards' bands during their sojourn in Paris. At a grand ball given by Wellington, when the Order of the Bath was conferred on Blücher and others, a traveller notes[10] that a military band (one of the Guards no doubt) played in the court of the hotel, but does not say anything of its performances, or even mentions its name. He speaks, however, of the pleasure he derived from listening to the celebrated band of the Emperor of Austria, which "surpassed . . . . any military orchestra" he ever heard.

---

[10] Scot, "Journal of a Tour to Waterloo and Paris, etc., in 1815."

CHAPTER VIII.

FORTY YEARS' PEACE.

"THE piping time of peace" which followed the Treaty of Paris (a stretch of forty years) gave the British army ample leisure to develop its taste for military music. No sooner had the war fever subsided, than attention was immediately directed to the regimental bands. Not that the War Office looked upon them with any favour, for bands were still in their eyes—so much "gingerbread." The only official sanction that the regulations of 1803 gave, was to permit one private soldier in each troop or company to be trained as a musician, and a sergeant to act as bandmaster. So strict were the authorities in this particular, that general officers of districts were required to report half-yearly that bands under their command were kept within the prescribed limit.¹ In 1822, the number of musicians for the regimental band is fixed at *ten*, not including "black men" or boys. The following year, the commander-in-chief was pleased to direct that "the establishment of each regimental band throughout the service shall be a sergeant (master) and *fourteen* "musicians." Here was progress for certain! Slowly but surely the government was finding out the value of the military band, and so we find that in 1837, they come to the view, that the formation of a "band of music" was "essential to the credit and appearance of a regiment," and tacitly insisted upon.

In spite of these instructions with regard to the strength of bands, ways and means were soon found to augment the regulation fourteen musicians to twenty-five or thirty.[1] This was managed by enlisting the services of men from the ranks, who were termed acting bandsmen, and in certain "crack" regiments, professional men were employed from civil life. With the exception of the Royal Artillery, no grants were made by the government for the support of these bands and most of the expense for their upkeep was borne by the officers, although in many regiments the "non-effective fund" still served for this purpose.[2] By a Horse Guards order of 1823, all officers were compelled to contribute to a fund for the support of the regimental band.[3] The band of the Royal Artillery was the only

---

[1] The band of the Royal Irish Artillery in 1801 consisted of about thirty-five members.—Browne, "England's Artillery-men." The Royal Artillery Band in 1812 numbered thirty-eight.—Farmer, "Memoirs of the Royal Artillery Band." The Coldstream Guards had a band of twenty-two in 1815.— Mackinnon, "Records of the Coldstream Guards."

[2] Grose, "Military Antiquities," 1801.

[3] This was fixed at twenty days' pay on appointment to any commission, and twelve days' pay per annum.—Campbell, "Dictionary of Military Science," 1830.

one officially recognised in the "Army Estimates," in which allowances were made for one bandmaster, one sergeant, two corporals and eighteen musicians (who received a special rate of pay) together with one hundred pounds per annum for the supply of music and instruments. It must not be thought that the Artillery were specially favoured. The explanation is to be found in the fact that prior to 1855, Horse Guards had nothing to do with this branch of the service, which was controlled by a Board of Ordnance.

At this time, the "grovelling superstition" as Gladstone called it, was abroad, that none but foreigners knew anything of musical matters, and so we find the majority of the bandmasters, and not a few bandsmen in our service were either Germans or Italians, a circumstance which reflected little credit on our national enterprise, to say nothing of assisting the popular delusion about "unmusical England."

Some officers actually selected their men personally when abroad, others would approach some distinguished musician to recommend bandmasters to them, just as a certain colonel of the Fourth Dragoon Guards importuned Mendelssohn for this purpose. The majority, however, were supplied by the various firms of instrument makers.

Although the government allowed a sergeant in each regiment as bandmaster, the latter invariably refused to be enlisted except perhaps in a corps whose officers had short purses, when an attested man meant less expense, and therefore insisted upon. Occasionally we find a bandmaster, who as a bandsman had attracted the attention of the commanding officer, and had been nursed and partially trained for the position. There was also a fair sprinkling of appointments from the ranks of the staff bands. Civilians reigned almost everywhere, and the incongruous spectacle of a conductor in civilian attire, directing a regimental band, would occasionally be seen. This class, both Englishman and foreigner alike, invariably declined to serve abroad, and terminated their engagement when a regiment was ordered there, looking out for a homecoming regiment with a vacancy.

In these days each band was formed on its own model using instruments of whatever kind or pitch the officers or bandmaster liked. The latter seems to have had a free hand in such matters. Indeed it was quite an understood thing, that when a new bandmaster took over his appointment, his first action was to condemn all the instruments in use, a custom which served the two-fold purpose of gratifying his own particular instrumental combination fad, and of rewarding the instrument maker to whom he owed his appointment, by ordering a new set of instruments. Regiments that had a substantial "band fund" would engage trained professionals, mostly from abroad, at big salaries, and obtained the best instruments procurable. "As a matter of course," says Kappey, "a certain rivalry soon arose between the different regiments as to the superiority of their bands. Whatever may be said of such a system, it is undeniable that the musical results were in many cases notable, and the service could boast (sixty or seventy years ago) of many superior bands "[4]

One striking result of the rapid development of military bands, was the adoption of one by King George IV, which he maintained in addition to the court orchestra. His predecessor, Thackeray's "dapper little George," had tried a similar thing, but it was not to be compared to the wonderful organisation of George IV, which was acknowledged in its time as "the finest in Europe." It was originally formed from the band of the Tenth Hussars, but in the course of time absorbed some of the finest wind instrumentalists in Europe. The bandmaster was Christian Kramer, "a musician of the very first order," says the old "Biographical Dictionary of Musicians" (1825). Among the "lions" of the band was Schmidt—allowed the first trumpet in Europe. "His flourish was the most terrific and appalling thing ever heard from a musical instrument." Rehns was one of the horns, and a marvel, and the King was extremely partial to him. Spellerberg was the principal oboe, and Eisert the solo clarinet. The first bassoon was Waetzig, afterwards bandmaster of the Second Life Guards, whilst Albrecht and Schroeder were principal alto and tenor trombones. The first serpent player was Andre, whose marvellous notes were the amazement of everybody. Kramer, the bandmaster, arranged a prodigious amount of music

---

Kappey, "Military Music."

for the band. From the most delicate song to the magnificent symphonies of Haydn, Mozart and Beethoven, and even the grandest of Handel's choruses, he preserved the bearing of each class throughout, and with so nice an attention to the particular cast of expression appertaining to each instrument. His knowledge of the effects of instruments was great.[5]

The band was instrumented thus:

4 Flutes.	2 Serpents.	1 Tenor Trombone.
3 Oboes.	4 Trumpets.	4 Bass Trombones.
12 Clarinets.	5 Horns.	2 Drums.
4 Bassoons.	1 Alto Trombone.	Total 42.

Not at all a bad combination for so-called "unmusical England." Of course it may be urged that this was a specially-selected organisation, and not to be taken as a specimen of English military bands of the period. Yet we shall see that some regimental bands were on as good a footing as the king's band, at least in numbers.

Here is the Royal Artillery band *circa* 1820:

2 Flutes.	3 Key Bugles.	1 Ophicleide.
3 Oboes.	2 French Horns.	2 Serpents.
11 Clarinets.	1 Alto Trombone.	2 Bass Horns.
3 Bassoons.	1 Tenor Trombone.	5 Drums, etc.
2 Trumpets.	1 Bass Trombone.	Total, 39.

Since Kastner, the historian of French military music, tells us that the Prussians and Austrians had incontestably the best bands at this time, we may take a glance at their construction and compare them with our bands and those of the French.

---

[5] "Biographical Dictionary of Musicians," 1825.

AUSTRIAN INFANTRY.
(1827.)
(AFTER SWOBODA.)

1 Piccolo, D flat.
2 Clarinets, A flat.
1 Clarinet, E flat.
9 Clarinets, B flat.
1 Bassoon.
1 Serpent.
2 Key Trumpets, E flat.
2 Trumpets, A flat.
2 Trumpets, E flat.
1 Trumpet, F.
1 Trumpet, C.
1 Trumpet, E flat.
2 Horns, E flat.
2 Horns, A flat.
2 Trombones.
1 Bass Trombone.
1 Side Drum.
Total 32.

FRENCH INFANTRY.
(1825.)
(AFTER ODIER.)

2 Flutes, F or E flat.
2 Clarinets, F or E flat.
4 Oboes.
12 Clarinets, B or C flat.
6 Bassoons.
2 Contra Bassoons.
2 Trumpets, F and E flat.
4 Horns, F and E flat.
2 Trombones.
Total 36.

Neither of these bands can compare as instrumental combination to those of the English, at least according to modern tastes. In the Austrian band there are only two bass instruments (a serpent and a bass trombone) and three tenor instruments (two trombones and one bassoon), whilst in the English band, a better balance is maintained with five bass instruments (four serpents and bass horns and one bass trombone) and five tenor instruments (three bassoons, one ophicleide and one trombone).

"The music that bands played at this period," says Dr. Niecks,[6] "consisted for the most part of arranged

---

[6] "Edinburgh University Historical Concert Programme," December, 1906.

music, chiefly operatic. Musical advertisements and
catalogues, as well as statements by contemporaries
support this view, which is strikingly and delightfully
illustrated by Mozart in the second act of his dramatic
chef d'œuvre, where Don Giovanni's musicians (two
oboe, two clarinets, two horns' and two bassoons, the
most complete and a very common combination) enter-
tain him at dinner with three extracts from popular
operas of the day, one from 'Le Nozze di Figaro.'
But although, undoubtedly, the arrangements enormously outnumbered the original compositions we may
safely assume that the musical conductors of the princes
and lesser nobles who had wind bands in their service
provided largely for their repertoire, of which, however,
comparatively little was printed, and much less than a
tithe has come to our knowledge."

The instrumental works of the great German symphony composers—Haydn, Mozart and Beethoven, do
not seem to have appealed to the military band
arranger. It was rather to the field of vocal music that
he turned. There we find transcriptions from the best
known oratorio choruses of Handel, and excerpts from
the masses of Haydn and Mozart. Dr. Turpin was of
opinion that it may even be questioned whether the glee
did not actually survive its original use, in an arranged
form, as a piece of display for military bands.

The favourite forms of military band music were
the "military concerto," "serenade" and "divertimento." The former sometimes took the shape of an

instrumental solo (clarinet, horn or flute), whilst the "divertimento" was a kind of "suite." Most of this music, I am inclined to think, came from France, as nearly all the specimens I have seen were published by Bisch, Paris, although a few bore the imprint of Bland, London.

Beethoven's military band scores, written a little earlier, are valuable for comparison here. I select his smallest and largest combinations:

MARCH IN F. (1809.)	MARCH IN D. (1816.)	
Piccolo in F.	2 Piccolos.	2 Bassoons.
2 Flutes, F.	2 Oboes.	Contra Bassoon.
Clarinet, F.	1 Clarinet, F	Tenor Trombone.
2 Clarinets, C.	4 Clarinets, C.	Bass Trombone.
2 Horns, F.	2 Horns, B Bass.	Serpent.
2 Trumpets, F.	4 Horns, D.	Side Drum.
2 Bassoons.	6 Trumpets, D.	Bass Drum.
Contra Bassoon.	Trumpet, B.	Triangle and Cymbals.
Side Drum.	Trumpet, G.	
Bass Drum.		

These give us an idea of German bands of the period.

It appears, however, from a letter of Beethoven's to Peters, the publisher (302 in the Wallace Collection) in 1823, that the composer thought his military band compositions would very likely be beyond the scope of German regimental bands, and suggests that some bandmaster be employed to arrange them for a smaller number.

Looking at the old time wind instruments in our museums, noting the primitive key mechanism of the wood wind, and the imperfect scale of the brass family, one can quite understand the startling effect which followed the introduction of the "valve," giving a complete and even scale to all brass instruments. It is true we had the key-bugle, ophicleide and bass horn, but their tone was very irregular and certainly did not blend well with other brass instruments. There was the trombone, which was chromatic, yet the more essential instruments—the trumpet and horn—were confined to the "harmonics." With the horn, a scale could be produced by a system known as "stopping," but uniform intonation had to be sacrificed, and it could not be safely practised on the march.

It was the invention of the "valve" that removed all these limitations. The question of priority in its introduction is too large a point to be entered into here. It is generally accepted that an Irishman named Clagget, was the first to conceive the idea. Two German musicians, Blühmel and Stölzel, brought out a successful application of two valves about 1813, to which a third was added by Müller, of Mayence. On its first appearance, a great many defects were found which made people rather suspicious of adopting it, and with the horn especially it was avoided because it was said to destroy the quality of the tone, a fallacy which gained credence for half a century. As we have seen with the clarinet, serpent, key-bugle and ophicleide, the military band was the first to take up the new idea. Kappey says: "It is due to the military bands that these improvements came into universal use." Even though the "valve" came from Germany, it laid dormant with them for some time. From 1818, it was taken up here and there in Prussia by regiments of cavalry and chasseurs, but little impression was created by the novelty, until a civilian musician, named Wilhelm Wieprecht (1802-72), applied it about 1828 to a family of brass instruments, which included an E flat soprano cornet (three valves), an E flat trumpet (two valves), a B flat tenor horn (three valves) and a B flat euphonium (three valves). Seven years later he designed the bombardon also with valves.

The introduction of the valve into England came about in a novel way. Of course it goes without saying that military bands had the honour of this. They were always the pioneers. About the year 1830, Earl Cathcart, the colonel of the Second Life Guards, went to St. Petersburg as Minister Plenipotentiary, and there he was very much struck with the playing of the band of the Imperial Guards. On inquiring of their organisation, he found that they played upon a rare contrivance known as a chromatic trumpet. The Earl was well in favour at court, and the Emperor of Russia was so gratified by the earl's high commendation of the performances of his Imperial Guard band, that he offered to present a set of these chromatic trumpets to the Earl's regiment in England, on condition that, whenever they played in public, the patent chromatic action should be covered, so as to keep the idea a secret. This was done. The "United Service Journal" of 1831, speaking of the "famous Russian chromatic trumpet band" of the

Second Life Guards, says it was the only one in England.

It could not be expected that the idea would remain long a secret. A bandmaster named Macfarlane soon applied two "Russian valves" to an instrument called a "cornopean" (now known as the cornet), which was brought out by Köhler, of London. The instrument then became universally adopted by our bands, and entirely superseded the trumpet and key-bugle. It was first introduced into the orchestra by Balfe in "The Maid of Artois" (1836).[7] The great world of the people's brass bands had its origin in these days, and Enderby Jackson, the famous brass band organiser, gives the date of the first band of any note, as 1833. This was established by Walker and Hardman, of York. The honour of forming the first brass band is also claimed by one Klussmann, the bandmaster of the Ninth Lancers.

---

[7] Barrett, "Balfe, His Life and Works."

CHAPTER IX.

REORGANISATION.

FROM 1830 to 1860, was an exciting period for military bands in England. Our "crack" regiments, now at the zenith of their extravagance in musical matters were spending enormous sums on their bands, for the rivalry between regiments was as keen as ever. It has been said that this system where bands were maintained by the officers, was more highly beneficial to military music, than that in vogue at the present time. Granted, as Kappey points out, that "the musical results were in many cases notable," one might ask how much harm was wrought in the midst of so much good? Buckle has shown in his "History of Civilisation," that the system of "patronage" under which art and literature existed in France at a certain period, hampered their development, since they only found expression so far as the necessities of their patrons required. Similarly, the system which obtained in England with regard to military bands, was nothing more than a brake on the wheel of progress, since regi-

mental bands were properly speaking under the patronage of the officers, and their excellence or otherwise
simply depended on the length of the latter's purses
and their musical tastes.

Among the best known of our "line" bandmasters
of the period were: Frost (1781- —); Blizzard, Duke
of York's School; King (? 1809-88), Fifth Lancers;
Owen (— -1867), Scots Greys; Cavallini (1807-73),
Fifty-fifth and Eightieth Regiments—"the Paganini
of the clarinet"; Longhi, Second Dragoon Guards;
Ruddland, First Dragoons; Oliver (? 1810-92), Twenti-
eth Regiment; Devine, Fourth Hussars; Emanuel,
A.R.A.M., (1819- —), King's Royal Rifles; Hay,
F.R.A.M. (1828- —); Eckersberg, Fourth Dragoon
Guards, composer of "Battle of Waterloo" fantasia;
Koenig, Eighth Hussars.

I have said that uniform organisation in our bands
was not thought of. The instrumental combination
and even the pitch, was a question which the officers or
bandmasters settled. It was therefore impossible to
combine several bands to a massed performance. A
similar state of affairs existed with continental bands.
In Germany, the first to clearly perceive the want of a
complete reconstruction was G. A. Schneider (1770-
1839), the Director-General of Prussian military music,
who worked at reform, according to the plan of one
Sundelin.[8] Then came Wilhelm Wieprecht (a civilian),

'Sundelin, "Die Instrumentirung für sammtliche Militär-
musikchöre," etc., 1828.

who recommended to the Prussian Dragoon Guards a plan for a brass band, all the instruments except the bugles and trombones being furnished with "valves"— quite an innovation This plan was adopted, and so successful were his efforts, that he was installed as teacher to the bands of the Cavalry Guards, which in time he reconstructed.

In 1838 he was appointed director of the bands of the Prussian Guards, and from that time dates the gradual reorganisation of Prussian bands. The bands of Wieprecht's reforms comprised :

INFANTRY.

2 Flutes.	2 Contra Bassoons.
2 Oboes.	2 Soprano Cornets, E flat.
1 Clarinet (High), A flat.	2 Alto Cornets, E flat.
2 Clarinets, E flat.	4 Trumpets.
8 Clarinets, B flat.	4 French Horns.
2 Tenor Horns, B flat.	2 Side Drums.
1 Euphonium.	1 Bass Drum.
2 Tenor Trombones.	Cymbals.
2 Bass Trombones.	Crescent (Bells).
4 Bombardons.	Total 47.
2 Bassoons.	

CAVALRY.

1 Cornettino, B flat.	8 Trumpets.
2 Cornettos, E flat.	1 Euphonium.
4 Cornets, B flat.	3 Bombardons.
2 Tenor Horns.	Total 21.

Kappey says that Wieprecht's methods "spread unto almost all European states and formed the basis of our present military music." England and France can scarcely be included in this very general statement. In these countries it is certain that the great Sax inventions formed the basis of their band reconstruction, and appears to have been a far more potent factor in the advance of the world's military music than Wieprecht's movement. Other noted bandmasters who assisted in Germany's band reforms were: Küffner (1776-1856), Neithardt (1793-1861) and Faust (1825-92).

Belgium too was caught in the tide of band reform. In 1846 a government commission was appointed to reorganise military bands, under Servais, of the Brussels Conservatoire. Their most famous military band was the "Guides" under Valentin Bender (1802-73), which was considered worthy of special mention by Kastner in his "Manuel Général de Musique Militaire," 1848. I append a list of this band at this period (1848):

1 Flute.	3 Bassoons.
2 Small Clarinets.	1 Russian Serpent.
2 Clarinets (B flat ?).	3 Bass Ophicleides.
2 Oboes.	3 Trombones.
4 Horns.	1 Bombardon.
3 Trumpets.	3 Drums, etc.
3 Cornets.	Total 32.
1 Bugle.	

In the Netherlands there had been a normal school for bandmasters since the beginning of the century, which since 1828 had been controlled by Joseph Snel (1793-1861).

Austria had also moved with the times. Prior to 1807, only the infantry and a few regiments of artillery possessed bands. But in this year they were granted to the cavalry, and in 1828 to chasseurs as well. Bands do not appear to have been official institutions with them. At any rate, bandmasters had no military standing, something like the position held by the same rank in our service, prior to the establishment of Kneller Hall. It was owing to the non-official position of these bandmasters that a "Pension Society for Austrian Army Bandmasters" was established in the middle of the last century. Austria's most noteworthy bandmasters of the period were: Starke (1774-1835), J. Sawerthal (1819-1903), V. H. Zavertal (1821-73) and Farbach.

The following is a specimen band of the Austrian infantry of the period (1848):[9]

1 Piccolo.	2 Bugles (Bass), B flat.
1 Flute.	6 Trumpets.
1 Clarinet, A flat.	4 Horns.
8 Clarinets, E flat.	6 Trombones.
4 Bassoons.	2 Bombardons.
2 Contra Bassoons.	Drums, etc.
4 Bugles, B flat.	Total 44.

In France, reorganisation of military bands followed closely after that of Prussia. In 1845 a special commission which included Spontini, Auber, Halévy, Adam, Onslow and Carafa among the musical experts, with Kastner as secretary, was formed to consider the question. They attributed the bad state of their military bands to: (1) The suppression of engaged professional men; (2) use of inferior instruments; (3) indifferent instrumental combinations; (4) insufficient number of executants; (5) the inferior position held by the latter.

---

[9] Kastner, "Manuel Général de Musique Militaire," 1848.

Several combinations were put before the commission; one, comprising the then existing organisation and others suggested by Carafa, the director of the Military School of Music, Adolphe Sax, the musical instrument maker, and Spontini.[10]   Here are specimens of the then existing organisations:

INFANTRY. (1845.) SIXTY-SECOND REGIMENT OF THE LINE.	CAVALRY. (1845.) SEVENTY-FOURTH REGIMENT.
1 Small Flute.	9 Cornets.
1 Small Clarinet.	3 Bugles, B flat.
12 Large Clarinets.	2 Trumpets.
3 Cornets.	1 Valve Horn.
2 Horns (Valve).	2 Néo Horns.
2 Horns.	2 Althorns (Clavicors).
3 Trombones.	2 Trombones.
6 Ophicleides.	6 Ophicleides.
6 Drums, etc.	Total 27.
Total 36.	

The instrumental combinations agreed upon by the commission, were based upon Sax's ideas, and the following organisations were admitted for the French Army under a decree dated July 31, 1845:

INFANTRY.	CAVALRY.
1 Small Flute in C.	2 Trumpets (Ordinary).
1 Small Clarinet in E flat.	4 Trumpets (Cylinders).
14 Clarinets, B flat.	2 Saxhorns, E flat.
2 Bass Clarinets, B flat.	7 Saxhorns, B flat.
2 Saxophones.	2 Saxhorns, A flat) instead of
2 Cornets (Cylinders).	2 Saxhorns, E flat) Horns.

---

¹⁰ Spontini suggested a fine combination. It is given in Grove's " Dictionary " (article, Wind Band).

2 Trumpets (Cylinders).
4 Horns (Cylinders).
1 Small Saxhorn in E flat.
2 Saxhorns in B flat.
2 Saxhorns in E flat (Alto).
3 Saxhorns in B flat.
4 Saxhorns, E flat (Contra-bass).
1 Trombone (Cylinders).
2 Trombones (Slide).
2 Ophicleides.
5 Drums, etc.
            Total, 50.

2 Saxotrombas.
2 Cornets.
1 Trombone (Cylinders).
3 Trombones (Slide).
3 Saxhorns (Baritone), B flat.
3 Saxhorns, B flat.
3 Saxhorns (Contrabass), E flat.
            Total 36.

Whilst the Sax organisation was in progress, the '48 revolution broke out, and the new government set aside the decree of 1845. Another plan for organisation was then issued, completely ignoring Sax. This called forth considerable comment. Berlioz wrote strongly on the matter in the "Journal des Débats," and the government was petitioned by many prominent musical and military men. In 1852, Albert Perrin issued his pamphlet on "The Organisation of Military Bands," which created considerable stir.[1] Sax was recalled, and the government issued the following in 1854, as the instrumentation for the bands of the Imperial Guards, and soon to the entire army :

INFANTRY.

2 Flutes or Piccolos.
4 Clarinets, E flat.
8 Clarinets, B flat.
2 Oboes.

CAVALRY.

1 High Soprano Saxhorn, B flat.
2 Soprano Saxhorns, E flat.
4 Soprano Saxhorns, B flat.

[1] It was translated into both English and Italian, and helped the cause of band reform in both countries.

2 Soprano Saxophones.
2 Alto Saxophones.
2 Tenor Saxophones.
2 Baritone Saxophones.
2 Cornets.
4 Trumpets.
3 Tenor Trombones.
1 Bass Trombone.
2 Soprano Saxhorns, E flat.
2 Soprano Saxhorns, B flat.
2 Alto Saxotrombas.
2 Baritone Saxhorns, B flat.
4 Bass Saxhorns, B flat.
2 Double Basses, E flat.
2 Double Basses, B flat.
5 Drums, etc.
           Total 55.

2 Alto Saxhorns, A flat.
2 Alto Saxotrombas, E flat.
2 Baritone Saxotrombas, B flat.
4 Bass Saxhorns, B flat.
2 Double Bass Saxhorns, E flat.
2 Double Bass Saxhorns, B flat.
2 Cornets.
6 Trumpets.
2 Alto Trombones.
2 Tenor Trombones.
2 Bass Trombones.
           Total 35.

This was the system which revolutionised the world's military music, due mainly to the "inventions" of Adolphe Sax. These "saxhorns" (patented in 1845) were immediately taken up by our regimental bands. First came the contrabass saxhorns, in E flat and B flat, which were called bombardons or basses, and superseded the serpents and bass horns. The bass saxhorn in B flat was then introduced as the euphonium or euphonion,[2] doing away with ophicleides. The baritone saxhorn in B flat was named simply the baritone or althorn, whilst the alto saxhorn in E flat retained its appellation, although under improved construction was designated the Koenig horn and tenor cor, and has to

---

[2] The original instrument still used on the Continent was of smaller bore. Phasey, a bandsman of the Coldstream Guards, designed the present wide bore in England.

some little extent reduced the importance of the French horn. Although mostly confined to the military band, the "saxhorn" family has been found a rare adjunct to the orchestral "brass" in the case of the euphonium and bombardon. The powerful tonal effects of the latter were recognised by Wagner, who employs it in the "Rheingold."

Nor had the brass family alone been improved upon. Boehm, Triebert, Klosé and others, had greatly increased the executive capacity of the "wood-wind" by their improvements and inventions. In 1839 Wieprecht constructed the "batyphone" to supply the bass to the clarinet family, but, outside Germany, it gained no permanent footing. The alto and bass clarinets began to be looked upon with favour from the days of Sax, and now have *completely* displaced basset horns, although Grove's "Dictionary," 1904 (article, "Arrangement"), on the authority of so distinguished a writer as Sir Hubert Parry, thinks otherwise. Berlioz regretted that so very beautiful an instrument as the alto clarinet was not to be found in all well-constituted orchestras. The bass clarinet has received more attention from composers—Auber, Halévy and Meyerbeer having written specially for it, notably the fine solo in the latter's opera, "Les Huguenots." Wagner also employs it in "Tristan und Isolde." The most important addition to wind bands was the saxophone, one of Sax's patents, registered 1846. This instrument, practically a clarinet of metal, gave a fresh tone colour to wind bands, and furnished a desired link between the reeds and brass. In this country its adoption has been slow, and it is only of recent years that it has been recognised in the "score." Although forming a "choir" of seven instruments, only four receive general acceptance, and in our service the E flat alto and the B flat tenor are usually considered sufficient to take a place in wind band music. Another French invention worthy of mention is the sarrusophone, designed by a bandmaster named Sarrus. The instrument is made in six or seven sizes similar to the saxophone and played with a double reed, but is not much used.

We have followed the reform of military bands on the Continent, and the rapid development of the resources of wind instruments, bringing such a wealth of tone colour that the wind band was considered an asset to the progress of art. We must now see how England fared at the time of Wieprecht's and Sax's movements with regard to organisation. An illustration of the composition of a first class band of the period, and that of an ordinary cavalry regiment, is appended:

ROYAL ARTILLERY BAND.'
(1839.)

1 Piccolo.
2 Flutes.
2 Oboes.

FOURTH LIGHT
DRAGOONS.
(*Circa* 1842.)

3 Cornets.
5 Trumpets.
2 French Horns.

Farmer, "Memoirs of the Royal Artillery Band," 1904.

3 Clarinets, E flat.
14 Clarinets, B flat.
4 Bassoons.
4 Trumpets.
3 Cornets.
2 French Horns.
4 Trombones.
1 Ophicleide.
2 Bass Horns.
2 Serpents.
4 Drums, etc.
          Total 48.

1 Kent Bugle.
1 Ophicleide.
3 Trombones.
1 Pair Kettledrums.
          Total 16.

Reform in English bands was not heralded by any government decree as in Prussia and France. It was brought about in two ways, firstly, by the establishment of a uniform instrumentation, and secondly, by the establishment of a military school of music. The former was not a pre-conceived scheme for reorganisation as we shall see presently. Printed music for military bands at this date was very scarce. The little there was came from the Continent, and this was arranged for instruments peculiar to their bands. Wessel had issued some band music between 1830-40, but the circulation was limited and the arrangement theoretical rather than practical. Those regiments that had bandmasters capable of composing or arranging were the best off, but their manuscripts were jealously guarded. All sorts of expedients had to be resorted to for the purpose of replenishing the regimental music library. If two regiments met, and their bandmasters were friendly, it was usual for them to inspect one another's repertoire, and make exchanges. This state

of affairs was clearly one to be remedied. One very
energetic bandmaster, Carl Boosé, of the Scots Guards,
had been striving for years to get someone to under-
take the publishing of military band arrangements, but
without success. Publishers were none too ready to
risk money on such a venture. Nothing daunted, Boosé
decided to be his own printer and publisher. In the
year 1845 he issued a selection from Verdi's "Ernani,"
which he not only arranged, but wrote the parts on
stone for lithographing, and printed them himself. His
publication soon attracted a good number of sub-
scribers, and immediately commended itself to Messrs.
Boosey and Co., who undertook the production
of a periodical issue of these works as "Boosé's Military Journal," 1846, appointing Boosé sole editor. So
great was the demand for this journal, that other publishers hastened to launch similar craft. Jullien brought
out a journal the following year under the direction of
Charles Godfrey, senior, the bandmaster of the Coldstream Guards. This was followed by an effort from
Schott and Co., edited by their kinsman, A. J. Schott,
bandmaster of the Grenadier Guards. Here were
three bandmasters of the foot guards editing rival publications. Of these, only two have survived, the first,
now known as "Boosey's Military Journal," and the
second which was acquired by Boosey's in 1857 as their
"Supplementary Journal." These journals practically
began the reform of our military music. Boosé's and
Jullien's publications being arranged on the same instrumental plan, bands found it necessary to adapt

themselves to it, and a fairly uniform combination throughout our service was the result, which formed the basis of our present system. So much for instrumental reform.

A greater evil still remained to be remedied—the system under which bands were raised and supported The chief objections to be urged against this were: (1) Bands were regimental institutions only; supported by their officers without any state aid (2) The employ-ment of civilian bandmasters and bandsmen over whom the authorities had little or no control. These we have dealt with at length, elsewhere. Reform in this direc-tion was delayed until well into the "fifties," and then was only brought about, by a clear demonstration of the defects of the prevailing system. It came with the Crimean War. Bands and music were forgotten all about in the hurry and scurry of mobilisation, and with many regiments there was every reason for it. The hired civilian bandmasters and bandsmen claimed their discharge, and many bands were broken up in this way. In short, the whole of our military music was completely disorganised.

At Scutari in 1854, the British troops, comprising the army of the east destined for the Crimea, held a grand review on the birthday of Queen Victoria. There were some sixteen thousand men on parade, and while their appearance and marching were perfect, and their cheer-ing deafening, our bands struck up "God Save the Queen," not only from different arrangements but in different keys! And all this, before the staff of the

allied army. No wonder a staff officer wrote afterwards that it "spoilt the fine effect" of the review. The
British officers must have felt ashamed, and no doubt
realised for the first time, what an amount of money
they had been paying for very indifferent music. Out
of about twenty regiments present, on this occasion,
only three or four had bandmasters with them. It has
been said that the Scots Greys was the only regiment
of the heavy cavalry that could boast of a band in the
Crimea. The French, on the other hand, maintained
their bands in a high state of efficiency throughout the
campaign, and it was their standing jest, that their
music at Inkerman did as much to drive back the Rus-
sians as the bayonets. (A doubtful compliment by the
way.) The French, however, did not admit such a
ridiculous system as that which found favour with us,
into their service. They had their "Gymnase de
Musique Militaire" for the training of their bands
which had existed since 1836, controlled first by Berr,
and then, 1838, by Carafa.

No one was more impressed with the disastrous state
of our military music, than a certain bandmaster named
James Smyth, a very practical musician, who was at the
head of one of our best staff bands—the Royal Artillery. Brimming over with ideas for the betterment of
our bands, he and another enthusiast, Henry Schallehn,
late bandmaster of the Seventeenth Lancers, and then
in charge of the Crystal Palace Band, had the temerity
to petition the Secretary of State for War on the question of band reorganisation. They pointed out the

necessity of improving the positions of bandmasters and bandsmen in the service, if we desired to reach the standard of continental bands. They further impressed upon the authorities that a bandsman was something more than a private soldier, that greater facilities should be given to further his musical education, and that he was capable of being trained as a bandmaster.

Schallehn had the good fortune to have the patronage of the new commander-in-chief, the Duke of Cambridge, under whom he had served in the Seventeenth Lancers. But the duke needed very little prompting concerning the state of our military bands. H.R.H. had campaigned in the Crimea, and marking the difference between our bands and those of the French, had already determined to remedy matters at the earliest opportunity.

The representations of Smyth and Schallehn had, however, some value as practical advice, especially on the points of training and education, and the need for a school for military bandsmen similar to the French, and the Duke at once took the matter in hand personally, by issuing a circular letter (dated September 26, 1856) which was sent to the commanding officers of regiments. It began: "H.R.H. The Commander-in-Chief, with a view to relieve regiments from the great expense now consequent upon the necessity of employing professional musicians, civilians, as masters of bands, has it in contemplation to recommend the establishment of a large musical class as part of the educa-

tion of boys sent to the Royal Military Asylum, and
for the instruction of persons sent from regiments to
qualify for bugle-majors, trumpet-majors and bandmasters, whose training would require special time and
attention." The initial outlay, it was thought, would
be about £500 or £600, and that about £1,000 per
annum would further be required to support the class.
The Commander-in-Chief said that the government
would only provide a building free, so that all other
expenses would have to be met by subscription, which
was estimated at £5 or £8 per annum, from each regiment, "but the result would be," said the Duke, "a
saving of expense to regiments and would tend to the
permanent efficiency of regimental bands." The scheme
was agreed upon by most regiments, and took practical
form by the establishment of a " Military Music Class "
at Kneller Hall, some ten miles from London, which
started on March 3, 1857. This was the inception of
the Royal Military School of Music, established to
train bandmasters who would be more directly con-
nected with their regiments than the previous civilian
conductors had been, and who would in all cases
remain with the band, either at home or abroad. It
was also meant to stimulate the acquisition of musical
knowledge amongst our own countrymen, by training
young men and lads as competent instrumentalists to
fill vacancies in the regimental band, and by holding
out to them, if they improved themselves and developed
sufficient talent, a prospect of obtaining remunerative

employment as bandmasters. This object has been kept steadily in view, and all the regulations which have been issued from time to time in connection with the school have been adopted with a view of furthering this object.[4]

---

[4] Marr, "Music and Musicians," etc., 1887.

CHAPTER X.

THE RENAISSANCE.

THE title of this chapter may appear somewhat
strange, in reference to wind instrumental bands.
But since it is obvious that music in general has
not progressed without reference to the other arts, it
follows that development of a particular phase of
music must rely to some extent upon its course being
shaped by other phases of the art. So that in dealing
with the renaissance of musical culture in England
which took place during the mid-nineteenth century,
we may take it that wind bands made a move with the
times. Mr. J. A. Fuller Maitland, in his "English
Music in the Nineteenth Century," has chosen the beginning of the second half of the nineteenth century
as the period of this revival. Yet throughout his three
hundred pages, he does not breathe one word concerning wind bands.[5] This is all the more remarkable when

---

[5] F. J. Crowest in his "Phases of Musical England," also
completely ignores the military band. Fortunately a new era
has dawned, and in the recently published "Musical England"
by W. J. Galloway, a chapter (based mainly on information
from the present writer's "Memoirs of the Royal Artillery
Band") is devoted solely to the subject.

we seek for some explanation as to how this revival was rendered possible, and to find the question untouched.

Wind instruments have always been the vehicle for the musical expression of the masses, from the time when the mediæval minstrel bagpiper discoursed on the village green down to the monster brass band festivals of to-day. A study of this phase of national music, would alone have furnished an explanation of this revival, for the art culture of this, as of every other epoch, can only be understood in reference to economic conditions; and it would not be difficult to show the correlation between the "music of the masses" of the nineteenth century, and the culture-conditions which produced it.

It will be gathered from what has already been said, that this musical renaissance in England found its expression in wind bands before any perceptible movement was shown in the so-called higher domain. One might say that it was the wind bands which fertilised the soil that was to bring forth the fruits of the renaissance.

They contributed the greatest service in the improvement of the attitude of the public towards music. The gigantic strides which were made by them cannot be paralleled in other branches of the art. The existence of the military band led to the formation of amateur bands and from the "thirties"—the starting point of the peoples' "brass bands"—to the great band festival of 1860, in which some fourteen hundred musicians took part, we see the movement assuming huge proportions, and spreading all over the country. With the military band, a more artistic combination, there was a manifestation of progress quite as startling, which had a still greater influence in moulding the tastes of the masses. The regimental band, which hitherto had rarely appeared in public, except on purely official duties, now came into great requisition, not merely for "society" functions, but for the open-air fêtes of the masses.[6] As the late Mr. Kappey pointed out, it was the military band which furnished in most cases the only medium by which the toiling multitude of the working classes—to whom the high-priced opera house or the fashionable concert-room were not accessible— could get any idea of musical progress.

Perhaps the first great public recognition of military bands in this country was when Jullien brought them into his monster concerts. The "Mons." as "Punch" called him, came from a country where the military band was held in high esteem, and heralded as a new phase of musical art which had yet to be developed, and moreover, had such men as Berlioz,[7] Spontini, Fétis and others as its sponsors. The first "grand military concert" given in this country was held at Chelsea in June, 1851, and the following were the chief items played by a massed band of some three hundred

---

[6] Reference to the writer's "Memoirs of the Royal Artillery Band" will bear out this point.

[7] Berlioz once applied for the post of director of the French Military School of Music.

and fifty performers, made up of the three regiments
of Household Cavalry, three regiments of Foot Guards
and the Royal Artillery, conducted in turn by their
various bandmasters :

(1) March, "Le Prophète"	*Meyerbeer*
(2) Overture, "Fest"	*Leutner*
(3) Overture, "Maritana"	*Wallace*
(4) Overture, "Camp of Silesia"	*Meyerbeer*
(5) Overture, "Euryanthe"	*Weber*
(6) "Ne touchez pas à la Reine"	*Boisselot*
(7) Selection, "Les Huguenots"	*Meyerbeer*
(8) Selection, "Lucia di Lammermoor" ...	*Donizetti*
(9) Selection, "Nino"	*Verdi*
(10) March, "Norma"	*Bellini*
(11) Quick Step	*Boosé*
(12) Waltz	*Karl Buller*
(13) Waltz	*D'Albert*
(14) "Quadrille of all Nations"	*Labitzky*

The "Times," commenting on the concert, said :

" The execution of these pieces was so admirable, the
ensemble so good, and the energy and decision of the
conductors so remarkable, that the unequivocal satis-
faction of the auditors was not to be wondered at. We
only regretted that with such splendid means so little
of real musical importance was effected. The overture
to 'Euryanthe' alone among the fourteen pieces presented was worthy of consideration as an artistic performance. Our military bands have reached a very
high degree of perfection in regard to the mere talent
of execution; but in other respects they have done little
or nothing to assist the progress of the art. If the
bandmasters who train them so zealously and well
would endeavour to instil into them some notion of

true music, instead of confining them almost wholly to
the most ephemeral productions, their influence would
be highly beneficial."

Note that our military bands had reached "a very
high degree of perfection." All the talk, however,
about instilling into the bandsmen some notion of true
music, was ridiculous! Most of the best performers of
the Guards' bands held good appointments in London
orchestras; and as for the Royal Artillery, the advice
was certainly ill-fitting, since this band had been giving
high-class orchestral concerts for over forty years, upon
the same model as the Philharmonic Society. Blame
for these "ephemeral productions" could not be laid
even against the bandmasters. Take, for instance,
Grattan Cooke, the bandmaster of the Second Life
Guards; surely it would be idle to pretend that a professor at the Royal Academy of Music, and one of the
best known musicians in London, had no higher tastes
than the "Quadrille of All Nations." The piece
selected by the "Times" as the only one worthy of
consideration was selected, arranged and conducted by
the bandmaster of the First Life Guards—James
Waddell, an ardent musician—who with the bandmaster of the Royal Artillery, William Collins, were
talked of in military band circles as progressive bandmasters, who made high-class compositions the chief items
on their programmes. At the funeral of the Duke of Wellington in 1852, the bands of Waddell and Collins were
specially mentioned by the papers, the reason being,
that whilst most bands were playing the "Dead

March" from "Saul," their bands were intoning the massive strains of Mendelssohn's "Antigone" and a movement from Spohr's "Power of Sound." These men, at any rate, had no tastes for "ephemeral productions."

During the early years of the Crystal Palace, grand concerts were given there by our staff bands. In those days, band concerts were in their infancy, and it was common to hear people say at the Palace: "There is no concert to-day, but the band is going to play!"

The first occasion of a military band going on a concert tour was in April, 1855, when the Royal Artillery band gave a series of high-class concerts in the north of England. This band was universally considered the finest in England at this period. In 1857 it was augmented from forty to eighty performers, and again in 1887 to ninety-three—the largest band in the service, which it has since remained. Here is the instrumentation of the Royal Artillery band during the reorganisation, together with other bands of the period.

ROYAL ARTILLERY BAND. (1857.)	106TH REGIMENT BAND. (c. 1860.)
2 Flutes and Piccolo.	3 Flutes and Piccolo.
4 Oboes.	1 Oboe.
4 Clarinets, E flat.	2 Clarinets, E flat.
22 Clarinets, B flat.	9 Clarinets, B flat.
2 Saxophones, E flat.	2 Bassoons.
2 Saxophones, B flat.	4 Cornets.
4 Bassoons.	2 Trumpets.
4 Cornets.	1 Althorn.
2 Trumpets.	2 Euphoniums.
2 Soprano Cornets, E flat.	3 Trombones.

2 Flügel Horns, E flat.
2 Flügel Horns, B flat.
4 French Horns.
2 Baritones.
4 Trombones.
2 Euphoniums.
4 Bombardons, E flat.
3 Drums, etc.
    Total, 71.

3 Bombardons.
3 Drums, etc.
    Total, 35.

17TH LANCERS.
BRASS BAND (MOUNTED).
(c. 1800.)

5 Cornets.
2 Trumpets.
3 Sax Horns.
2 Baritones.
2 Euphoniums.
3 Trombones.
2 Bombardons.
1 Drum.
    Total, 20.

ROYAL ARTILLERY
BRASS BAND (DISMOUNTED).
(1863.)

1 Soprano Cornet.
1 Cornet.
5 Chromatic Bugles.
5 Flügel Horns.
6 Tenors, E flat.
3 Baritones.
2 Euphoniums.
3 Bombardons.
    Total, 26.

The combination of the 106th Regiment is a fair specimen of the average infantry band of the period. Since the publication of the military band journals, wind instrumental combinations had become stereotyped. Very rarely, except in the case of staff bands, was the rule deviated from. In the Royal Artillery band we may note the employment of saxophones, flügel horns and soprano cornets, instruments imparting fresh tone-colour, but with the exception of the first named, they have been little encouraged in our military bands.

In 1863, Albert Perrin's brochure on the "Organization of Military Bands" (1852), which had stirred both

France and Italy into band reform, was published in English. In a special preface, the author addressed the Commander-in-Chief on the "inefficiency" of our line bands, and condemned our military music whole-sale. What the direct effect was I cannot say, but it is remarkable that from the year 1863 dates the official recognition of army bands in this country.

As I have already pointed out, with the exception of the Royal Artillery and the Royal Military College, bandmasters were not officially recognised. The regu-lation simply permitted a sergeant to act as such. In 1851-2 the "Army Estimates" allowed bandmasters for the Duke of York's and the Royal Hibernian Schools who had hitherto been paid from another source. This was certainly a step in the right direc-tion, for these two institutions played no small parts in the progress of our military music during the last century. Nothing, however, was done for the line regiments until 1863, when the Government allowed a "sergeant bandmaster" to each regiment of infantry, and a "bandmaster" to each regiment of cavalry, placing them on an equal footing with sergeant-majors. Staff bands, like the Guards, were not taken into con-sideration, probably for the reason that, being station-ary, they had always been able to maintain good bands and bandmasters, and had never been affected by the evils under which the marching regiments laboured.

The staff bands, i.e., those of the Household Cavalry, Foot Guards, Royal Artillery and Marines, have

18

always been the finest wind instrumental combinations in England, and as such may justly be considered the pioneers in all matters of military music.

The Foot Guards' bands enjoyed (and still do so) many special privileges which were not extended to any other branch. They resided out of barracks, and only appeared in uniform when on duty, or at band engagements. The Royal Artillery and Royal Marines being "double-handed," supplying a full "string orchestra" as well as a "wind band," were playing the best music of the day.[8] It is not to be wondered at that these staff bands should be such superior organizations to those of "line" regiments.

Being stationary and, with the exception of the Marines, always resident in London, these bands have been able to retain the services of a better class of musician than the "line" bands. With the Guards and Artillery, their members were, for the most part, professional musicians, engaged in the best concert and theatre orchestras in London. In earlier days, when our great metropolis could not boast of the number of fine educational institutes for music as it does to-day, these bands were looked upon quite in the light of wind instrumental conservatories, which promising players joined, practically to complete their musical

---

[8] The Royal Artillery Band has been "double-handed" since its formation in 1762. The Portsmouth Marines raised its string band in 1853 and the Chatham Marines in the early "sixties." The Royal Engineers band have had an orchestra since its formation in 1856.

training, and to ensure for themselves an entry into the best circles of the profession.

During the greater part of the nineteenth century nearly all the leading "wind players" were military men, and Guardsmen mostly. Here is a run of clarinettists, the principal artists of their day: Mahon (1755-1834), Willman (1784?-1840), and Lazarus (1815-95)—all from the army. Lesser "stars" were Hopkins, *primo* clarinet at the opera, etc., Cavallini— the "Paganini of the clarinet," and Cadwallader Thomas. Among famous bassoonists were "Ashley of the Guards," of the old-time Handel Festivals, Wotton, the foremost performer of his time, Waetzig, of the Queen's private band, and John Winterbottom, of Jullien's and Mellon's concerts. The most eminent trumpet players of the century were Harper and F. McGrath, to say nothing of Jules Levy and Howard Reynolds, the cornet *virtuosi*. Reinagle, subsequently a distinguished 'cellist, Callcott, the father of the composer, Jarrett and Thomas Mann, were all well-known horn players. I may recall among oboists, Grattan Cooke, a professor at the R A M., William Crozier and George Horton. Phasey and Guilmartin were renowned ophicleide and euphonium players, whilst William Winterbottom, R. H. Booth, Thos. Colton and Innes, were among our best performers on the trombone

The wave of patriotism which swept over England at the time of the Crimean war and after, gave a decided fillip to military bands. The Volunteer movement (1859) especially helped in this direction. In

Scotland so great was the enthusiasm for bands, that contests were organized in 1862-3 and 1865, "with a view of increasing the efficiency of Volunteer and other bands in Scotland."[9] This general repair of bands brought about the birth of two more "staff" bands— the Royal Engineers' Band (1856) and the Royal Artillery Brass Band (1856).

The former corps had raised a small band in the "thirties," a very poor, unofficial affair. The new band was quite a fresh organization and comprised thirty-six performers. The Royal Artillery Brass Band, which carried off first prize at the Crystal Palace band contest of 1871, was re-instrumented in 1878 as a full military band, and called the Royal Artillery Mounted Band. This became a very fine combination, and gave weekly symphony concerts (purely as a military band), playing the entire symphonic works of Beethoven, Mozart and Haydn, quite a novelty in those days. It was disbanded in 1887-8, although it provided a nucleus for a band of the same name, which exists to-day.

The instrumentation of the original band just before its dissolution was:

1 Piccolo.	2 Sarrusophones.	4 Euphoniums.
1 Flute.	7 Cornets.	5 Trombones.
2 Clarinets, E flat.	2 Trumpets.	5 Bombardons.
16 Clarinets, B flat.	4 Horns	3 Drums, etc.
4 Bassoons.	1 Baritone.	Total, 57.

[9] Marr, "Music and Musicians."

In 1870 two more "staff" bands were raised, the Royal Horse Artillery (under J. A. Browne), which was merged in the Royal Artillery Mounted Band in 1878, and the Royal Marine Artillery, under John Winterbottom.

The Military School of Music must also be allowed its share in the development of military music during the renaissance. For whatever may be said against the early bandmasters from the school, there can be no question of the work which this institution did in the training of the bandsmen. When it opened its doors on March 3, 1857, a staff of only four professors, including the director of music, then called the "resident instructor," was employed. At first the school gave little promise of success. The most serious trouble which beset the school was the meagre support afforded it. Regiments were free to subscribe toward its maintenance, or not, as they thought fit. And, of course, there were many regiments who had no desire to avail themselves of Kneller Hall, preferring the old style of civilian bandmaster and training their own bandsmen. Even in later years, when compelled to have a Kneller Hall bandmaster, some regiments employed civilian "conductors." Another set-back was caused by the appointment of Schallehn as director of the school, who, we are told, had "no exceptional ability." After two years in office, he was dismissed.

Despite the ill-luck which attended the school at the outset, there happened to be at the head of affairs a very ardent musician, Lieut.-Col. F. L. Whitmore, who was the first commandant of Kneller Hall.[10] It was this officer who laid the lines upon which the school was to be conducted, in regard to regimental matters and interior economy. Great improvements have since been made by successive commandants, but the general system still obtains, thus proving the correctness of Col. Whitmore's judgment. The real work of directing the training of embryo bandmasters and bandsmen devolved of course upon the director of music, and in selecting a successor to Schallehn, Col. Whitmore was fortunate in fixing upon a very clever musician and an excellent teacher in the person of Carl Mandel. During Mandel's appointment the school got into full swing. The professors, which at the inauguration only numbered four, had now been increased to ten, and were selected from the best of their class in England. The famous Lazarus taught the clarinet, Barret was oboe professor, Phasey was responsible for the tenor brass instruments, and Mann had charge of the French horns. Whilst among the other teachers, were Carl Zeiss (trumpet), late professor at Brussels Conservatoire, Albert Hartmann (flute), afterwards bandmaster 17th Lancers, and the first bandmaster in our service to take the degree of Doctor of Music (Oxon.), and Sir Arthur Sullivan's father, who taught the bass brass instruments.[1]

---

[10] There was a Colonel Stephens in appointment before him, but only for a short time.

[1] It is worth while remarking that three of our great national composers were cradled, so to speak, in the atmosphere

Although only a semi-official institution, the Military School of Music came under the War Office control (apparently) in 1867, and the material assistance which this institution was giving to the whole movement of military band reform soon became apparent to the authorities, for in 1872, the government gave its first grant toward its support, followed three years later by complete control being assumed. It then became imperative that all bandmasters should pass through Kneller Hall, though existing arrangements were not to be interfered with.

Among the leading staff bandmasters of the day were: James Smyth, of the Royal Artillery; Boosé, of the Royal Horse Guards; Waddell and Waterson, of the First, and Froenherdt, of the Second Life Guards; Dan Godfrey, of the Grenadiers; Fred Godfrey, of the Coldstreams; Charles Godfrey (Jun.), of the Scots Guards; Kappey, of the Chatham Marines; and William Winterbottom, of the Woolwich and Plymouth Marines. These are the men to whom all credit must be given for the part they played in the English musical renaissance of the mid-nineteenth century.

There were some good men in the "line" bands who also deserve mention: W. Miller, of the First Rifle

---

of military music. Balfe's first teacher (like Beethoven's) was an army bandmaster (of the Kerry Militia), whilst his first lessons in instrumentation came from another bandmaster, named Meadows. The father of W. V. Wallace was bandmaster of the Twenty-ninth Regiment, whilst Sullivan's father was bandmaster of the Royal Military College band.

Brigade, who wrote the march, "I'm Ninety-Five"; John
Hartmann, of the Fourth Regiment, Twelfth Lancers,
etc., the composer of "An Evening in Berlin"; Crowe,
of the Fourteenth Light Dragoons, of Covent Garden
Promenade Concert fame; Basquit, of the Fifty-eighth
Regiment, who wrote the waltzes, "Kleine Camarad"
and "Pastoral Songs"; Bonnisseau, of the Scots Greys,
who composed the fantasia, "Robert Bruce"; Relle, of
the Twenty-eighth Regiment, well known for his dance
music, "Farewell Waltz" and "Spanish Beauty Quadrille"; J. Hecker, of the Eighty-fourth Regiment, composer of the fine waltzes, "Zephir Lufte," "Perlen der
Gedanken" and "Die Schwebenden Geister"; Tamplini, of the Forty-eighth, Ninety-sixth and Twenty-
fourth Regiments, the author of the "Bandsman";
Foster, of the Ninth Regiment, who wrote the overture,
"Rob Roy"; Morelli, of the Seventy-sixth Regiment, a
fine arranger; J. Sidney Jones, of the Fifth Dragoon
Guards (father of the composer of the "Geisha"),
founder of the Yorkshire Training College of Music.
They mostly belonged to that old class of civilian
bandmasters long since passed away, one of whom
J. Hamilton Clarke describes in his "Two Chorus
Girls": "A fair musician, an enthusiast in the art, and
a perfect gentleman, he was worshipped by the men,
whose studies were a matter of personal interest to
him, and whose difficulties he always smoothed for them
as if he were a college tutor and they undergraduates."

When our bands were making great strides, several
of those on the Continent were in the grip of parsi-

monious governments, and were suffering accordingly.
In 1863, Belgium instituted a commission, under
Gevaert and Victor Mahillon, to inquire into their military bands,[2] but little seems to have been effected by
way of reorganization. Austrian bands fell on evil
times altogether. Here is an infantry band of 1860,[3]
quite an inferior organization to that of 1848 (see
Chapter IX).

1 Piccolo.	2 Horns.
1 Clarinet, A flat.	2 Tenor Horns.
2 Clarinets, E flat.	2 Euphoniums.
4 Clarinets, B flat.	4 Trombones.
2 Cornettinos, B flat.	4 Bombardons.
2 Cornettos, E flat.	3 Drums, etc.
2 Cornets, B flat.	Total, 35.
4 Trumpets.	

In 1868 bands for cavalry, chasseurs and artillery
were entirely suppressed in Austria. There were some
first-rate musicians among Austrian bandmasters of the
period, including Gung'l, Kéler Béla, P. Fahrbach,
Nemetz and Zimmermann.

France, the great herald of band reform, suffered
worse than Austria.

When the war broke out with Italy, French bands
were reduced to forty for infantry and twenty-five for
cavalry. Then in 1867, cavalry bands were suppressed
altogether, which was ratified by a decree of 1873,
which also ordered infantry bands to be kept at forty.
The French Military School of Music ("Gymnase de

[2] "Military Service Journal" (U.S.A.).
[3] Grove's "Dictionary" (article, Wind Band).

Musique Militaire "), which had existed since 1836, was abolished in 1856, the government arranging for a military music class to be started at the Conservatoire, under the professors from the "Gymnase de Musique Militaire." This was suppressed soon after the Franco-Prussian war, although Sax, who had charge of the class, offered to continue his services without any payment.[4]

Prussia, with Wieprecht still at the head of affairs, continued in good form, and was able to demonstrate its superiority by carrying off the first prize at the great international contest held at Paris in 1867. Among the adjudicators were Georges Kastner, Ambroise Thomas, Delibes, Von Bülow, Félicien David, Hanslick, etc. The test piece was the overture, "Oberon," and the result :[5]

AWARD	STATE	BAND	STRENGTH	CONDUCTOR
First	Prussia	Massed Bands of two Regiments of Guards		Wieprecht
,,	France	" Garde de Paris "	56	Paulus
,,	Austria	Seventy-third Regiment	76	Zimmermann
Second	Bavaria	First Infantry Regiment	51	Siebenkäs
,,	Russia	Mounted Guards	71	Dorfeld
,,	France	Mounted Guides	62	Cressonois
Third	Holland	Massed Bands of Chasseurs and Grenadiers	56	Dunkler
,,	Baden	Grenadier Regiment	54	Burg
Fourth	Belgium	Massed Bands of Guides and Grenadier Regiment	59	Bender
,,	Spain	First Engineer Corps	64	Maimo

[4] Neukomm, "Histoire de la Musique Militaire," 1889.
[5] "La Musique Populaire," 1867.

England would permit none of its bands to take part in the contest, although a special application was made by the French government for the leading band of the day, the Royal Artillery Band, under Smyth, to enter the lists.

In 1882 this band came under the baton of Cavaliere Ladislao Zavertal, the greatest musician the British service ever possessed, who raised it to perhaps the foremost position in the annals of the military band. Here is the band as it was constituted at the close of its famous chief's career:

2 Piccolos.	2 Koenig Horns.
2 Flutes.	3 Althorns.
4 Oboes.	5 Trombones.
4 Clarinets, E flat.	4 Euphoniums.
29 Clarinets, B flat.	9 Bombardons.
4 Bassoons.	3 Drums, etc.
13 Cornets.	Total, 91.
7 French Horns.	

Another band which shared laurels with the former, was that of the Grenadier Guards, under the conductorship of Dan Godfrey, the most popular bandmaster of his day. This band took part in the great festival at Boston (U.S.A.) in 1872, being the first British band to leave its native shores.

Here is the instrumentation of this band in 1888, when at the height of its fame:[6]

1 Piccolo.	6 Cornets.
2 Flutes.	2 Trumpets.
2 Oboes.	4 Horns.

'Marr, "Music for the People," 1889.

4 Clarinets, E flat.
14 Clarinets, B flat.
1 Clarinet, E flat Tenor.
1 Clarinet, B flat Bass.
2 Bassoons.
1 Contra Bassoon.

1 Baritone.
3 Trombones.
4 Euphoniums.
6 Bombardons.
8 Drums, etc.
                    Total, 57.

The numerous international exhibitions which have been held in England, have given splendid opportunities to military bands, not only to our own, but to those of other countries. Among the most important of the latter which have visited England are the French Garde Republicaine, the Belgian Guides and the New York Twenty-second Regiment (Gilmore's), all most artistic combinations, the latter especially. Here is the instrumentation of Gilmore's band (1878) and the Belgian Guides (1888):[7]

GILMORE'S BAND.

2 Piccolos.
2 Flutes.
2 Oboes.
1 Clarinet, A flat.
3 Clarinets, E flat.
16 Clarinets, B flat.
1 Clarinet, Alto.
1 Clarinet, Bass.
1 Saxophone, Soprano.
1 Saxophone, Alto.
1 Saxophone, Tenor.
1 Saxophone, Bass.
2 Bassoons.
1 Contra Bassoon.
1 Cornet, Soprano.

BELGIAN GUIDES.

1 Piccolo.
1 Flute.
2 Oboes.
2 Clarinets, E flat.
12 Clarinets, B flat.
4 Bassoons.
2 Cornets.
5 Trumpets.
2 Bugles.
4 Horns.
1 Saxhorn, Soprano.
2 Saxhorns, Alto.
1 Saxhorn, Tenor.
2 Baritones.
4 Euphoniums.

In Kalkbrenner's "Die Organisation der Militairmusikchöre aller Lander" (1884) full particulars of the organization of the world's military bands are given.

4 Cornets, B flat.	6 Trombones.
2 Trumpets.	1 Contra Bass.
2 Flügel Horns.	3 Bombardons, E flat.
4 French Horns.	2 Bombardons, B flat.
2 Horns, E flat Alto.	3 Drums.
2 Horns, B flat Tenor.	Total, 60.'
2 Euphoniums.	
3 Trombones.	
5 Bombardons.	
4 Drums, etc.	
Total, 66.'	

Here I must cry halt! for I do not intend, for obvious reasons, to encroach upon the "present." However, I would like to conclude with a reference to a work recently published, "Musical England," by W. J. Galloway, in which a chapter is devoted to military bands. The author says "that at the present moment no other country has more good military bands than England." He also lays stress, and justly too, upon the important position our bands have now assumed in the musical life of this country. "The employment of military bands at places of public entertainment," says Mr. Galloway, "enables them to appeal to larger audiences than can be reached even by the leading metropolitan orchestras. At exhibitions and fêtes, as well as at private gatherings, they have enormous opportunities for influencing public taste, and if in turn public taste has reacted on them, it is only fair to say that the musicians of the army in the past—and still more in the present—have taken full advantage of the educational openings put before them."

---

8 Grove's "Dictionary" (article, Wind Band).
9 Marr, "Music for the People."

If, as our social prophets tell us, the to-morrow belongs to the democracy, then the recent enormous growth and increasing recognition of the military band (which truly reflects the tastes of the masses) may be taken as a sign of the times, and augurs well for the future.

STAFF BANDMASTERS.

(1800 TO PRESENT TIME.)

INCLUDING BANDS OF FIRST LIFE GUARDS, SECOND LIFE GUARDS, ROYAL HORSE ARTILLERY, ROYAL HORSE GUARDS, ROYAL ARTILLERY (WOOLWICH), ROYAL ARTILLERY MOUNTED, ROYAL GARRISON ARTILLERY (DOVER, PORTSMOUTH AND PLYMOUTH), ROYAL MARINE ARTILLERY, ROYAL ENGINEERS, GRENADIER GUARDS, COLDSTREAM GUARDS, SCOTS GUARDS, IRISH GUARDS, ROYAL MARINE LIGHT INFANTRY (CHATHAM, PORTSMOUTH, PLYMOUTH AND WOOLWICH), AND DIRECTORS OF ROYAL MILITARY SCHOOL OF MUSIC.

BARKER, LEONARD (1852- —). Bandsman, Royal Artillery, 1870. Bandmaster, Scots Greys, 1882; Second Life Guards, 1889-95.

BATTISHILL, PERCY F. Bandsman, Sixtieth Rifles, 1884. Bandmaster, Queen's Regiment, 1896; Royal Garrison Artillery (Dover), 1904.

BIES, —. Bandmaster, First Life Guards, *circa* 1820.

BILTON, J. MANUEL (1862- —). Bandsman, Royal Artillery. Bandmaster, Seventeenth Lancers, 1891; Royal Horse Guards, 1903. Composer of Symphony in E flat, cantata, "The Wreck of the Hesperus," overtures, "Petruchio," "Ulysses," "Kossuth," etc.

BLANEY, JAMES (?). Bandmaster, Grenadier Guards (*circa* 1815).

BOOSÉ, CARL (1815-69). Bandsman, German Army. "One of the best clarinet players of his day" (Marr, "Music for the People"). Bandmaster, Ninth Lancers, 1841; Scots Guards, 1842; Royal Horse Guards, 1859. Decorated with Hessian "Order of Merit." Editor of Boosey's "Military Band Journal."

BROWNE, JAMES A. (1838- —). Bandsman, Royal Artillery, 1848. Bandmaster, Royal Horse Artillery, 1870-8. Editor and sub-editor "British Bandsman," "British Musician" and "Orchestral Times." Author of "England's Artillerymen," 1865, etc. A well-known arranger, "From East to West," etc.

CLARKE, JAMES P. (—-1889). Bandsman, Sixty-first Regiment and Seventh Hussars. Bandmaster, Forty-seventh Regiment; Seventh and Eleventh Hussars; Thirty-sixth, Eighty-third, Forty-third and Fifty-fourth Regiments; Royal Irish Constabulary, 1872; Scots Guards, 1875-87. (Erroneously stated to be a Mus.Bac. in Baptie's "Musical Biography.")

COLLINS, WILLIAM (1815-86). Bandsman, Royal Artillery. Bandmaster, Royal Artillery, 1845; Royal Bucks Militia, 1854; Royal Engineers, 1856-65.

COOKE, HENRY A. M. (1809-89). Educated R.A.M. Principal oboe, Philharmonic and other orchestras. Professor, R.A.M. Bandmaster, Second Life Guards, 1849-56. Composer of operettas, songs, etc.

COUSINS, CHARLES (1830-90). Bandsman, First Life Guards, 1848. Bandmaster, Second Dragoon Guards, 1863. Director of Military School of Music, 1874-90.

CUNNINGHAM, ALBERT J. (1868- —). Bandsman, Royal Artillery. Bandmaster, Royal Irish Rifles, 1896; Royal Garrison Artillery Band (Dover), 1903-4. Conductor, Londonderry Philharmonic Society.

DENMAN, JAMES. Bandmaster, Coldstream Guards, *circa* 1815.

DUNKERTON, HENRY T. Bandmaster, First Munster Fusiliers; Scots Guards, 1893-1900.

EARLE, —. Bandmaster, Royal Marines (Portsmouth), *circa* 184-.

ELEY, CHRISTOPHER. Bandmaster, Coldstream Guards, 1785-18—.

ELRINGTON, —. Bandmaster, Grenadier Guards, *circa* 1794.

ENGLEFIELD, JOEL (1844- —). Bandsman, Eighteenth Hussars, 1858. Bandmaster, Eighteenth Hussars, 1867; First Life Guards, 1890-1903.

EVANS, ROBERT G. (1868- —). Bandsman, Royal Artillery, 1885. Bandmaster, Highland Light Infantry, 1898; Royal Garrison Artillery Band (Plymouth), 1903.

FLUX, NEVILLE (1878- —). Educated R.A.M. Conductor, Mayfair Orchestral Society, 1900. Bandmaster, Royal Engineers, 1905. Conductor, Rochester Choral Society. His works include a Symphony in G, tone poem, "The Legend Beautiful," "Four Characteristic Dances," numerous overtures and smaller pieces.

FRANKLIN, CHARLES, Second Lieutenant (1861- —). Bandsman, Munster Fusiliers, 1875. Bandmaster, Royal Irish Rifles, 1890. Director of Music, Egyptian Army, 1894. Director, Royal Naval School of Music, Eastney, 1907.

FROENHERDT, C. F. (18— -90). Bandmaster, Sixty-fourth Regiment, 1845; Ninety-fourth Regiment, 1845; Second Life Guards, 1856; Royal Marines (Plymouth), 1872. Inspecting bandmaster, H.M. Training Ships, 1874.

GODFREY, CHARLES (1790-1863). Bandsman, Coldstream Guards, 1813. Bandmaster, Coldstream Guards, 1825-63. Member of King's Band, 1831. First editor of Jullien's "Military Band Journal."

GODFREY, CHARLES, M.V.O., F.R.A.M. (1839- —). Educated R.A.M. Bandmaster, Scots Guards, 1859; Royal Horse Guards, 1869-1903. Commissioned Second Lieutenant 1899. Member, Royal Victorian Order, 1903. Professor, R.C.M. and Guildhall School. Editor of "Orpheus Band Journal."

GODFREY, DANIEL (1831-1903). Educated R.A.M. Bandmaster, Grenadier Guards, 1856-96. Appointed honorary Second Lieutenant, 1887. The first bandmaster in our service to receive the commissioned rank. Professor of military music at the R.A.M. Composer of the waltzes, "Guards," "Hilda," "Mabel," etc.

GODFREY, FREDERIC (1837-82). Bandsman, Coldstream Guards, 1856. Bandmaster, Coldstream Guards, 1863-80. Editor of Chappell's "Military Band Journal."

GREEN, BENJAMIN, M.V.O., Second Lieutenant (1853- —). Bandsman, Eighth Hussars, 1865. Bandmaster, Tenth Hussars, 1879; Duke of York's School, 1888; Royal Marine Artillery, 1897. Second Lieutenant, 1911.

GRIFFITHS, SAMUEL C. (1851-96). Bandsman, Royal Scots, 1866. Bandmaster, Royal Scots, 1872; Royal Military College, 1890. Director, Royal Military School of Music and Second Lieutenant, 1890. Composer of overture, "Hermohn," motet, "God be Merciful unto Us." Author of the "Military Band" and "Hints on the Management of Army Bands."

HAINES, FREDERIC, L.R.A.M. (1870---). Bandmaster, Royal Lancaster Regiment, 1894; First Life Guards, 1903-8.

HALL, C. W. H., Second Lieutenant, M.V.O. (1858---). Bandsman, Twelfth Lancers. Bandmaster, First Royal Dragoons, 1884; Second Life Guards, 1889.

HARDY, W. Bandmaster, Grenadier Guards, *circa* 1830; Scots Guards, 1838. Retired 1842.

HASSELL, CHARLES H. (1866---). Bandsman, Ninety-fifth Regiment, 1878. Bandmaster, Fourth King's Royal Rifles, 1892; Irish Guards, 1900.

HEUVAL, WILLIAM VAN DEN (1836---). Bandmaster, Ninth Regiment, 1858; Seventh Hussars, 1859; First Life Guards, 1879-90.

HOBY, CHARLES, A.R.C.M., L.R.A.M. Educated R.C.M. Chief Bandmaster, Punjaub Frontier Force, 1889-90; Natal Royal Rifles. Bandmaster under London School Board. Organist, St. Luke's Church, South Kensington. Bandmaster, Royal Marines (Chatham), 1907. Composer of songs, etc. (Novello).

HOLLAND, EDWARD (1853---). Bandsman, Rifle Brigade, 1865. Bandmaster, Forty-eighth Regiment, 1878; Scots Guards, 1887; Norfolk Artillery, 1893 (?).

HOPKINS, EDWARD (*circa* 1778-1860). "The first clarinet player of his day" ("Brit. Mus. Biography"). Bandmaster, Scots Guards, *circa* 1797-1838.

KAPPEY, J. A. (1826-1906). Bandmaster, Eighty-ninth Regiment, 1848; Royal Marines (Chatham), 1857. Composed an *opéra bouffe*, "The Wager," cantata, "Per Mare, per Terram," musical comedy, "The Moonlight Serenade," etc. Author of "History of Wind Instrumental Bands." Editor for Boosey and Co.

KREYER. Bandmaster, Royal Marines (Portsmouth), 186-(?)-84.

LAWSON, JAMES (1826-1903). Bandsman, Royal Artillery, 1839. Bandmaster, Royal Artillery Bugle Band, afterwards the Royal Artillery Mounted Band, 1856-87.

LEE, CHARLES (1863---). Bandsman, Twentieth Hussars, 1883. Bandmaster, Fourth Dragoon Guards, 1886; Royal Garrison Artillery (Portsmouth), 1908.

MAANEN, J. C. VAN (1827-99). Educated Hague Conservatoire. Bandmaster, Fifty-second Regiment; Royal Scots, 1851; Bengal Artillery, 1856; Scots Guards, 1869; Royal

Irish Constabulary, 1875. Musical director of Lyceum and Prince of Wales Theatres, London. Professor of wind instruments at Royal Irish Academy of Music.

MCKENZIE, GEORGE (1780-1865). Bandsman, Royal Artillery, 1795. Bandmaster, Royal Artillery, 1810-45.

MANDEL, CARL (?-1874). Director of Music, Kneller Hall, 1859-74. Author of "System of Music," "Treatise on the Instrumentation of Military Bands," etc.

MILLER, GEORGE, Second Lieutenant, M.V.O., Mus.Bac. (1853-—). Bandsman, Sixteenth Regiment. Bandmaster, Sixteenth Regiment, 1874; Royal Military College, 1880; Royal Marines (Portsmouth), 1884; L.R.A.M., 1882; Mus.Bac (Cambridge), 1892. Composer of "Voyage in a Troopship," etc. Is a Chevalier of the "Ordre Militaire de Notre Dame de la Conception."

MILLER, GEORGE, Junior, L.R.A.M. (18—-—). Educated *Kapellmeister Aspiranten Schule*, Berlin. Bandsman, King's Royal Rifles, 1896. Bandmaster, King's Royal Rifles, 1898; Royal Garrison Artillery (Portsmouth), 1903; First Life Guards, 1908.

NEWSTEAD, WILLIAM (1826-75). Bandsman, Royal Artillery, 1837. Bandmaster, Royal Engineers, 1865-71.

NEWTON, JOHN W. (1873-—). Bandsman, Norfolk Artillery, 1886. Sergeant Trumpeter (Bandmaster) Sligo Artillery, 1894. Bandmaster, Second Durham Light Infantry, 1904; Royal Marines (Plymouth), 1910.

ROGAN, J. M. Second Lieutenant, M V.O., Mus.Doc. (Hon.), (1852-—). Bandsman, Eleventh Regiment, 1867. Bandmaster, Royal West Surrey Regiment, 1882; Coldstream Guards, 1896.

ROGERS. Bandmaster, Royal Marines (Chatham), 18—-1857.

SAWERTHAL, JOSEF R. (1819-1903). Educated Prague Conservatoire. Bandmaster, Austrian Army. Musical Director Navy and Marine, 1850. Court Capellmeister to Maximilian, Emperor of Mexico. Entered English service as Bandmaster Fourth Regiment, 1868, and Royal Engineers, 1871 (not 1867 *vide* Baptie). Retired 1891. Composer of opera, "Pastzrka," 1847. Decorated by Emperor of Austria and Napoleon III.

SCHALLEHN, HENRY. Bandmaster, Seventeenth Lancers, 184-. Conductor, Crystal Palace Band, 1854. Director of Music, Kneller Hall, 1857-9.

SCHNUPHASS, G. Bandmaster, Royal Artillery, 1802-10.

SCHOTT, A. J. Bandmaster, Seventy-ninth Regiment Grenadier Guards, 1844-56.

SIBOLD. Bandmaster, Grenadier Guards, 1838-44.

SIMS, HENRY (1858- —). Bandsman, Fourth Dragoon Guards. Bandmaster, Cavalry Depot, Canterbury, 1885; Royal Artillery Mounted Band, 1887.

SMYTH, JAMES (1818-85). Bandsman, Nineteenth Regiment. Bandmaster, Nineteenth Regiment, 1841; Royal Artillery, 1854-81.

SMYTH, THOMAS. Bandmaster, Royal Marines (Woolwich), 1856-7; Royal Marine Artillery, 1859.

SOMMER, JOSEF, Second Lieutenant, M.V.O. Educated Cologne Conservatoire. Bandmaster, Seventeenth Regiment, Twenty-sixth Regiment; Hyderabad Contingent, 1890; Royal Engineers, 1891-1905.

STRETTON, ARTHUR, Major, M.V.O. (1863- —). Bandsman, Royal Artillery, 1875. Bandmaster, Cheshire Regiment, 1893. Director, Royal Military School of Music, 1896.

STRETTON, EDWARD C. (1871- —). Bandsman, Royal Artillery, 1886. Bandmaster, York and Lancashire Regiment, 1900. Director, Royal Naval School of Music, 1903; Royal Artillery, 1907.

THOMAS, CADWALLADER (1838- —). Bandsman, Coldstream Guards, 1853. Bandmaster, Duke of York's School, 1870; Coldstream Guards, 1880-96.

THOMSON. Bandmaster, Royal Marines (Woolwich), 183 -54.

TUTTON, JAMES R. One of the founders of the "Society of British Musicians." Bandmaster, Royal Horse Guards, 18—-1859. Composed "Dramatic Overture," "March of the Men of Kent," etc.

ULRICCI. Bandmaster, First Life Guards, *circa* 1830.

WADDELL, JAMES (1797-1879). Bandmaster, Eightieth Regiment, 1817; First Life Guards, 1832. Composer of overture, "Fair Maid of Perth," etc.

WAETZIG, JOHN G. "An excellent bassoon player" (Grove). Member of the court bands of George IV, William IV and Victoria. Bandmaster, Second Life Guards, 183 -49. Sergeant Trumpeter, Royal Household, 1875.

WATERSON, JAMES (—-1893). Bandsman, First Life Guards. Bandmaster, First Life Guards, 1863 (?). Bandmaster to Viceroy of India, 1878. Editor of "British Bandsman." Composer of overture, "Sidonia," and a fine wind quintet, etc.

WEYRAUCH, JOHN. Bandmaster, Coldstream Guards, *circa* 1800.

WIELE, FRIEDRICH. Bandmaster, Royal Artillery, 1777-1802. Dragoons and Sussex Militia.

WILLIAMS, ALBERT, M.V.O., Second Lieutenant, Mus.Doc. (Oxon), (1864-—). Bandsman, Sixty-first Regiment, 1877. Bandmaster, Tenth Hussars, 1888; Royal Marine Artillery, 1892; Grenadier Guards, 1897. Mus.Bac., 1891; Mus.Doc., 1906. Composer of oratorio, "Elisha," "Heloise" and other overtures. Is a member of the Order of the Crown of Prussia.

WILLMAN, THOMAS LINDSAY (1784-1840). "The most celebrated of English clarinettists" (Grove). Army bandsman, principal clarinet at the Opera, Philharmonic, etc. Professor, Royal Academy of Music. Bandmaster, Coldstream Guards, *circa* 1816-25.

WINTERBOTTOM, FRANK (1861-—). Professor of Music, Dulwich College, and conductor of musical societies. Bandmaster, Royal Marines (Plymouth), 1890-1910.

WINTERBOTTOM, HENRY. Bandmaster, Seventh and Eighteenth Regiments; Royal Marines (Woolwich), 1854-6.

WINTERBOTTOM, JOHN (*circa* 1817-97). Famous bassoon player. Bandmaster, Royal Marine Artillery, 1870; Artists' Rifle Volunteers, 1892.

WINTERBOTTOM, THOMAS (*circa* 1819-69). Bandsman, Royal Horse Guards. Bandmaster, Royal Marines (Plymouth), 1851-69.

WINTERBOTTOM, WILLIAM (*circa* 1820-89). Bandsman, First Life Guards. Principal trombone, Philharmonic, Opera, etc. Bandmaster, Royal Marines (Woolwich), 1857; Royal Marines (Plymouth), 1869.

WOOD, FREDERICK W. (1864-—). Bandsman, Fifth Lancers. Bandmaster, York and Lancashire Regiment, 1890; Scots Guards, 1900.

WRIGHT, JOHN, Second Lieutenant (1854-1907). Bandmaster, South Lancashire Regiment, 1877; Royal Marines (Chatham), 1892.

ZAVERTAL, LADISLAO, Commendatore, M.V.O., Second Lieutenant (1849- —). Educated Naples Conservatoire. Theatre conductor, Milan, 1869. Conductor musical societies, Glasgow, 1871. Bandmaster, Royal Artillery, 1881-1906. Composed operas, "Tita," "Una Notte à Firenze," "Mirra," two symphonies, etc. Second Lieutenant, 1898. Member of Royal Victorian Order, 1901; Order of the Crown of Italy; Ernestine Order for Art and Science.

ZOELLER, CARLI (1840-89). Educated Royal Academy of Art, Berlin. Bandmaster, Seventh Hussars, 1879; Second Life Guards, 1887-9. Composed lyrical drama, "Mary Stuart," cantata, "Qui sedes Domine," three masses, "Ave Maria" for eight voices. Author of "Art of Modulation" and "The Viole d'Amour."

INDEX.

Printed by The New Temple Press, 17 Grant Road, Croydon.